Planning and the Urban Community

Planning and the Urban Community

Essays on Urbanism and City Planning presented before a Seminar Sponsored by the Joint Committee on Planning and Urban Development of Carnegie Institute of Technology and University of Pittsburgh

Edited by Harvey S. Perloff
Director, Program of Regional Studies, Resources for the Future, Inc.

With the assistance of Edward Foster and Perry Norton

Carnegie Institute of Technology

University of Pittsburgh Press

86101

Library of Congress Card Catalog Number: 60-16547
© 1961, University of Pittsburgh Press
Printed in the United States of America

These essays have been published

with the assistance of the Wherrett Memorial Fund

of The Pittsburgh Foundation

Foreword

There are few occasions that lend themselves so naturally to a broad review of a field of professional study as does one in which the possibility of establishing a new training center is being considered.

At the beginning of 1958, University of Pittsburgh and Carnegie Institute of Technology began to examine the desirability and feasibility of setting up a jointly-sponsored planning school. The faculty committee, under the leadership of Dean Donald C. Stone and Dean Norman L. Rice, which had been given the responsibility of developing proposals, invited me to advise them on the most appropriate manner for carrying forward a program of education, research, and advisory services in "planning and urban development." I accepted this invitation as an opportunity to make a contribution under the Resources for the Future program of assistance to universities in the field of regional studies. I asked Perry Norton, who had been until recently Executive Director of the American Institute of Planners, to collaborate with me in this consulting task.

Given the very great difficulties involved in establishing a program which required the active support not only of a number of different disciplines but of two separate universities with their own unique approaches and traditions, we urged a careful, step-by-step clarification of the many philosophical and operational issues involved in establishing a joint planning program. Among other recommendations we suggested a faculty-student seminar to which outstanding persons from planning and related fields would be invited to discuss major problems in urbanism and planning. Such a seminar could serve to provide a valuable overview of a complex professional field in a period of rapid development; it could bring light to bear on the actual and potential relationship of various fields of study to planning, the nature of professional planning activities, the unresolved issues of planning practice and planning education, and possible future forms of urban planning.

This volume brings together the papers presented before the joint planning seminar during the fall of 1958, and some of the discussion related to these papers. The materials are organized into three sections. The papers in Part One focus on the subject which is the central concern of city planning—the urban community —and indicate what we know or may come to know about it. Part Two deals mainly with various approaches to organizing city planning; its place within the governmental hierarchical structure, how it is or may be organized horizontally across the many governmental units that make up the metropolitan region, and its relationship to urban political dynamics. The papers in Part Three probe the nature of urban planning activities, present and future, and the implications for planning education.

Neither in the invitations to the seminar speakers nor in the editing of the papers was any attempt made to direct the presentations into a preconceived mold. It seemed much more appropriate—and attractive—to let the individual styles and the nature of the subject matter give form to the papers. As a result, the original presentations varied from the reading of carefully prepared formal papers, at one extreme, to loosely organized panel discussions at the other. The essays as they appear in this volume reflect this variation. Rather careful editing of the papers was, in a sense, substituted for a preconceived format. Where the comments of the discussants or the question-and-answer materials offered interesting and fresh materials, these have been included—in some cases, after quite liberal rewriting by the editors. Throughout, the emphasis was on the suggestive and insightful materials, and the aim was to get each of the three parts to hold up as sensible units, rather than to have each of the individual essays appear as a full and finished statment of the particular topic.

The final product can be said, then, to *characterize* the planning field rather than provide a text for it. This itself is of interest, particularly for the educator and for the professional in the field. The current stage of development of a professional field can be expected to influence in many ways the things that are written about it at any given point in time. It is clearly significant, then, that this volume of essays on urban planning appears at a time when the city planning field in the United States would seem to be in a late-adolescent stage of development. A rather distinctive personality is already apparent and yet there is the expected floundering around for direction; in other words, there is the wonderful (and to older persons—or professions—puzzling) confusion of adolescence just preceding the firm strides of early manhood. There is a contagious, youthful hopefulness coupled with young-old cynicism; the reading of romantic poetry joined with the reading of Machiavelli (or in city planning terms, the urge to design the esthetically satisfying total community and at the same time the talk of working within the "realistic" framework of politics and selfish interests).* There is the easy hurt, the tendency for overstatement at precisely the points where there is the least assurance —and always the search for direction.

* By contrast, I suspect one would find little "reading of poetry" among the membership of the more mature professional groups.

Foreword

It is useful to be aware of the stage of development of the field, not only because it gives special meaning to a collection of this sort, but also because it helps to highlight the fact that there is an exciting, open road ahead of urban planning. There is plenty of scope for great achievement.

I want to express my appreciation to Edward Foster, Planning Associate of the Institute of Local Government, University of Pittsburgh, and to Perry Norton for their invaluable assistance in organizing the seminar and in editing the papers for this volume. Thanks are due Fred Utevsky of the Pittsburgh City Planning Commission, who served as reporter for the seminar, and whose notes were of great value to the editors.

I also wish to thank the Joint Committee on Planning and Urban Development of the two institutions, and particularly Deans Rice and Stone, for their enthusiastic support of our various recommendations. If the committee can achieve the seemingly impossible task of organizing a two-university school of planning of distinction, it will surely have a special place in the annals of professional education. Much as I value this by-product of the effort to establish a planning program in Pittsburgh, I hope that it turns out to be only a first item of a long line of significant planning literature emerging from this important center of learning.

Harvey S. Perloff

Preface

Harvey S. Perloff has achieved a remarkably impressive degree of unity and coherence in this collection of essays and comments by some of the nation's leading planners and noted scholars in the field of urban studies.

The University of Pittsburgh and the Carnegie Institute of Technology, sponsors of the joint seminar at which these papers were presented, are deeply appreciative to Dr. Perloff both for his editorial skill and for his planning of the program in which such an outstanding group of experts participated. We thank each member for his contribution. We know that all readers of this volume will join with us in expressing appreciation to Resources for the Future, Inc. for its generosity in making the services of Dr. Perloff available for this project.

It would not have been possible to publish this volume without the financial assistance of the Wherrett Memorial Fund of The Pittsburgh Foundation.

We hope that this successful venture will point the way to similar cooperative undertakings between the two universities.

NORMAN L. RICE
Dean, College of Fine Arts
Carnegie Institute of Technology

DONALD C. STONE
Dean, Graduate School of
Public and International Affairs
University of Pittsburgh

Pittsburgh, Pa.
1 October 1960

Contents

xiii

xiv

Introduction

Understanding the Urban Community

It cannot quite be said that city planning is a field in search of a subject, and yet it is true that the topic of its central concern—the urban community—is not readily defined. This difficulty, however, planning shares with all the disciplines and professions that are importantly concerned with urbanism—and its problems. Thus, planning inevitably joins forces with other fields of study in a search for understanding of the urban phenomenon, first—in historical sequence—easily labeled the City, then the Metropolis, and now increasingly (and not so easily) labeled the Urban Region.

The essays in this section, in different ways, probe the nature of modern urbanism and its many facets. The authors here are clearly not blind men touching the various individual parts of the elephant and crying out that they thereby know the nature of the beast. There is evident throughout a sensitivity that what is being dealt with is a highly complex phenomenon with delicately interrelated parts, that an evolutionary process is at work and one must see it in all of its dynamism.

As is true of the other two parts of the volume, the subject of this section is far from exhausted; rather there is a highlighting of a few significant and intriguing elements. And yet the breadth and complexity of the subject emerges fully. We are shown the urban community as a *civilization*—as a way of life and as the product of that way of life, as a "physical utility for collective living," and as a work of art; as a *society* (as a community)—encompassing a vast network of human and institutional interrelationships, changing its character with numbers and quality and purposes and movements of persons and groups; as an *economy*— serving a whole set of complex functions and as the crossroads and collecting point for endless flows of goods, capital, and workers. We are introduced to the city also as a political phenomenon, but this phase is mainly developed in Part Two of the volume.

In another vein, we are shown the tremendous *forces* at work in shaping the form—and problems—of the urban community. The pervading force of rapidly changing technology emerges sharply. Powerful economic, cultural and artistic, social, and political forces, which are often national and even international in scope, are seen as changing the character and the pathologies of the urban scene.

In yet another cut at the problems of trying to understand the urban entity, we see the metropolis or urban region in terms of *spatial and land-use arrangements*, a vast mosaic, some of which would seem to be frozen, and yet which is always subject to change by way of new uses, shifts in transportation and communication patterns, and of course rebuilding itself. However, this facet, which is of such central concern to city planning, is treated only peripherally—a leaving for later discussion. Here and there, however, some highly suggestive concepts are introduced, as in Smuts's treatment of designing to capacity, or in Rice's characterizations of urban esthetics, or in Hoover's analysis of the spatial requirements of various economic activities, or in Meier's references to the implications for planners of the far-reaching technological changes under way.

While the emphasis throughout the section is on *understanding*, each facet of the urban community which is brought forth either explicitly or implicitly introduces what might be thought of as a companion challenge—for human endeavor generally and for planning more specifically. Thus, the concept of *urban civilization* suggests the notion of *enrichment;* there is so much to be done to have our urban communities reflect our righer cultural achievements. Is the planning problem of the urban university, for example, really one of surrounding decay and redevelopment, or is it a problem of how to build the university into the urban fabric as a true "center" of learning and cultural achievement? Shouldn't we look for ways of bringing our greatest architectural and artistic achievements into the center of the city where more people can see them more frequently—isn't it time, in other words, that the CBD truly became the Central Business *Plus Cultural* District?

In the same way, to take only one other example, an understanding of *urban economy,* with its stress on the importance for business of communications and access joined with an equal stress on the costs of congestion, suggests a challenge for planning in devising bold experiments which will help provide some firm answers for achieving optimum communication and access with minimum congestion. It is the challenge of facing up to unknowns and uncertainty in the most sensible way we know how—through experimentation. This is far from the one-best-way approach and is, in fact, an approach that can help turn planning into a great human *and* scientific adventure.

Part One

Understanding the Urban Community

Chapter One

The Economic Functions and Structure of the Metropolitan Region

by Edgar M. Hoover

Professor of Economics, University of Pittsburgh

How would one answer if asked by a man from Mars, "Just what are these 'Metropolises' you have on your planet, and what purpose do they serve?"

An economist might immediately point out that a metropolis is, among other things, a big cluster of rather diverse economic activities. He would find it a bit harder to explain *why* we have all these metropolises. For instance, he might start explaining that they occur in this and that location because of certain obvious "natural advantages." There is New York's splendid natural harbor; there are coal deposits as a basis for much of the industry of the Pittsburgh region; and so on.

This explanation, it seems to me, misses a major point —one that I wish to stress; namely, what it is that metropolises have *in common*. We can't explain them as a class on a basis of these individual natural-advantage

3

factors. What they have in common, I submit, is *the economic advantage of intensive contact among a diversity of individuals and firms that is made possible by the high density of business and population and by the special facilities for communication that develop within a metropolis.*

This factor is fundamental; for with this advantage of contact, we should have cities and metropolises arising even if there were no differentiation in terms of natural features at all. Even on a uniform plain, we should still get urban clusters.

So our central question is why this advantage from concentration of economic activity? We are probably all familiar with what has been said about the advantages of large-scale production within a single plant, or production establishment. We know, for instance, that there is the important principle of division of labor. The efficient division of labor requires, though, that the plant be big enough to occupy fully even the most specialized of the various kinds of machine or manpower units it employs. So, the size of the plant has to be a sort of the least common multiple of the various minimum efficient sizes of the kinds of equipment and skills you have. Still another principle, sometimes referred to as "massing of reserves," is essentially like insurance. With a large volume of operations, there may be increased probability that various individually unpredictable interruptions and irregularities in supply or demand will "average out," so that inventory needs and margins of capacity do not need to be relatively so big as in a smaller-scale operation.

We know that a single establishment generally does not fully exploit the possible technical economies of size because other factors limit its growth. Maybe the limit is the financial resources or the managerial capacity of the operator, or the fact that the business is new and hasn't yet grown up. Maybe it is distribution costs, limiting its geographical market area. Now the attraction of an urban cluster is that, in a sense, production establishments can have it both ways. Without being big themselves, they can *indirectly* obtain some of the advantages of large-scale production, by contracting out parts of the operation to specialized firms, so in a sense division of labor among firms substitutes for division of labor within a single firm. For example, there are in the fashion garment industry, in a big city, specialized firms that do nothing except supply buttons. They can handle this particular operation on a bigger scale and more economically (here largely because of the massing-of-reserves principle) than any of their customers could by themselves. So some economies are related to the size not of the plant, but of the cluster of related plants.

When we try to trace out the various economies arising in urban locations, we find that they ramify into other and still other industries, and eventually involve a good part of the whole urban economy. For example, one of "external" economies of a location in a central business district is the availability of rental space—flexibility in getting space when you want it and no more nor no less than you want. Another is the availability of freight forwarding and parcel services. They give "fractional" service and yet the freight forwarder passes on some of the economies he makes by shipping in large quantities. There are many other types of specialized business services, and, of course, there is the big diversified labor market.

We have, then, three levels of "scale" economies. First, in the individual plant; secondly, in the cluster of plants in an industry in one locality; and thirdly, in the whole urban production setup, cutting across industry lines. The important point is that economies of all these types are contingent upon close, quick contact. They normally cannot work over any great distance. The fashion garment manufacturer will say he must be right in the garment district. One of his many reasons is that if a machine breaks down, he wants to be able to get immediate repair or replacement. Similarly he wants to be able to expand his work force at practically no notice.

Moreover, metropolises are also centers of display for style goods. They are centers of public administration. They are centers of "economic administration" in the big office buildings that are the hallmark of central business districts. And they are cultural centers. One can say that in all of these functions there are "scale economies," without stretching the concept too far.

Perhaps that is enough about why the metropolis *exists*. Let us look inside it and see what we can say about its structure, and the why of that.

First, there is the obvious fact of central concentration within the metropolis. Everything seems to pile toward the middle. Why? In the most primitive sort of situation we can imagine, we can see the seeds of that phenomenon. Suppose we have people living in some type of tribal organization. We shall assume there is a need for contact in the sense that the tribal society can function as a unit provided everybody is within, say, a mile of every other member of the tribe, so that he can see him every day if he needs to. If distances are any greater than that, the tribal organization will not function. This imagined society is a very primitive analogy of a modern metropolitan community.

Now, if the people are dispersed evenly, what is the maximum size of the integrated community? A circle, one mile in diameter, the people at opposite edges being at the extreme distance apart. Such a size, of course, severely limits the economies of scale. But we notice that even in this situation, location at *the center* has a unique advantage. The center is the point from which the average distance to all the other points is least. We might call this the initial or "geometrical" advantage of a central point as such.

This advantage soon gets reinforced. One fine day a member of this tribe has a brilliant idea: why not establish a gathering place in the center, to which everybody comes every day—a clearing house for contacts. The idea is adopted. What happens? Immediately the possible area of this community quadruples. We now have a circle of one mile *radius*. Everybody can see everybody by just walking a mile (or less) to the central point. The next thing, of course, is that beaten paths get established leading into this central point. Transportation becomes more developed, easier, quicker, and cheaper in a radial direction than crisscross, as is still generally the case in modern metropolitan transportation. So the center acquires cumulative advantages as a site for any kind of activity that requires extensive contact among the members of the community.

Of course, not all activities can be there, even though it is the ideal location. The prime space gets rationed, in our system by the mechanism of competitive rent. The user willing to pay the biggest rent gets the choicest central location and others go farther out. Each activity is placed on the basis of its relative need for space as against access, plus the ability to pay for such space.

This is the schematic picture that von Thünen developed for agricultural zones around a central market town. A very similar model, for the zones of land use

7

in metropolitan areas, is known as the Burgess Zonal Hypothesis.

An obvious first step toward reality is to allow for differences in transportation cost and speed in various directions: so we do not really expect the pattern of land uses to look like the concentric rings of the cross-section of an onion, but more like a starfish, with projections along routes of rapid transportation (or perhaps, in such topography as is to be found in a place like Pittsburgh, an octopus would be a better simile).

However, an actual metropolitan land-use pattern strikes us as much more scrambled than the zonal hypothesis would imply even after allowing for irregularities in transport and topography. Let me suggest a few reasons for that.

The zonal hypothesis rests on a very much simplified theory of location. It assumes that only two things matter—space requirements and the need for access—and that access means access to *everybody in the metropolis.* This simple formula does not always fit.

For instance, there are some urban activities that deal primarily with the outside world. Good access for them means essentially cheap and convenient transport into and out of the area. The best spot for such an activity then would not be in the center where all the transit lines converge and daytime population is most dense, but somewhere in the transport terminal zone. If they ship or receive by water, then they are drawn toward the waterfront, otherwise, to rail or truck terminal areas. Many kinds of manufacturing for large regional or national markets behave in this way. Less and less of it is in downtown central business zones.

Again, the best position for some firms depends essentially on a *clustering* of a particular complex of related activities. One thinks in this connection of fash-

8

ion garment manufacturers or jewelry dealers. These clusters do indeed most often seem to settle somewhere within the central business district. But there is nothing inevitable about that, unless other factors call for a central location. For instance, a clustering of research establishments, laboratories, and the like can derive important advantages from close contact, but there is no particular reason why such a cluster has to be in the central business district. The people mainly involved in the contacts live predominantly in the suburbs and such a cluster can be and often is suburban.

Still other activities are tied to fixed natural features. They may have to be on the water either for transport or to use the water in large quantities, as for instance an electric power station does. Or a brick plant has to have its clay pit. These activities are obviously not attracted especially to the center of the metropolitan area.

Then there are activities tapping some specialized part of the labor market which may draw them toward an off-center focus. Plants using primarily engineers, for instance, may be drawn primarily to suburban locations on a belt highway. Thus Route 128 around Boston has attracted an impressive array of electronics plants. A survey of their labor experience showed that such location aided in getting and holding professional and executive staff, and that any problems in labor supply were at the lower pay levels.

Finally there are, of course, those "local" activities that have to split up and serve from any one location only a piece of the metropolitan area market, because they have to be close to the customer and customers are scattered over the whole area. Examples are retail trade and consumer services and some local business services like banks. Activities like this are attracted to

9

population, but that can mean any of three things. For some the attraction is toward where people *live:* e.g., establishments that service houses and household equipment. For others the attraction is toward where people *work:* e.g., business services or noonday eating places. For still a third class, the market is the *pedestrian.*

In short, many specific activities deviate from the simplified centripetal-centrifugal locational scheme underlying the concentric zone "hypothesis"; so we get a much more complex pattern. There are further schematic theoretical patterns that to some extent recognize these other factors: for instance, the "sector" and "subcenter" concepts of metropolitan structure. These are essentially refinements of or supplements to the zonal hypothesis.

Now, to get to a different and rather pressing question: what major changes have been affecting and are likely to affect the structure of American metropolises?

One is the steady trend of increased real income and leisure. This means that people can exercise and do exercise more effective demands for desirable living space. They can bid higher for space, and space is more worth having. Desirable living space or plenty of open ground around you may not mean very much if you work a twelve-hour day, six days a week. It means a lot if you work a thirty-five-hour week. It will mean still more in the future.

Another big change, more important still, is the mass use of automobiles. The whole rationale of the metropolis, I have argued, is personal contact. The way people get about and make contact is crucial for the shape of the metropolis. Their travel within the area is accomplished more and more in private automobiles. The automobile offers fast direct transportation with much lower required minimum route density than previous means of transport: that is, we can have a much finer and more extensive network of routes with the automobile simply because a passable road costs less to build than a rail line. This means that a tremendous area of new possible sites are opened up for both work and residence that were not economically accessible in the pre-automobile era. The effect is cumulative. The suburban factory has many new sites open to it because it can use trucks. At the same time, these sites are possible because employees can get there in their cars. Their cars, moreover, make it possible for them to live off the route of mass transportation.

We can see this happening in terms of the map of land uses in metropolitan areas. I mentioned the starfish or an octopus pattern as still typical. When we open up the areas between the tentacles by automobile transport, we see a less fingery, more even, but also more dispersed pattern of land development. (The starfish develops webbed feet.)

Here is a statistic to illustrate this process. In 1925, only 1 per cent of the built-up residential area in the twenty-two-county New York metropolitan region was more than a mile from a rail station. This meant of course, that a tremendous area "between the tentacles" was not built up, but became available as mass automobile transportation entered the picture.

One thing about the automobile is that for the first time it makes it possible for the commuter to get someplace from home without first having to walk. Suburban developments in the pre-automobile stage were built up on what we now consider rather high density because everybody had to be within walking distance of the rail or transit stop. By contrast, subdivisions more re-

11

cently laid out for car-equipped commuters have very much larger lots and low density.

The other side of the coin is that the automobile uses a great deal of space per person moved. This affects particularly the central city. It becomes more difficult for people to get into or through the central area. It is interesting to notice that the number of people traveling into Manhattan shows no trend of increase in recent years, in spite of the terrific growth of the New York metropolitan region as a whole. The growth in trip-destinations has all been outside Manhattan. Central city areas generally have lost through the automobile some of their former access advantages and the suburbs have gained in convenience of access advantage, not to the center but to each other. General cross-suburban traffic is really feasible for the first time.

The result is that a good many activities have left the central districts. Take the Pittsburgh area between 1948 and 1954. The Pittsburgh central business district has a diminished percentage share in the total metropolitan area business in nearly all lines of trade. The picture is similar in most metropolitan areas. Manufacturing has moved outward as well as consumer services and a good deal of the office work that does not call for daily contact.

Some activities have remained as centralized as ever though. The center is still the best place for all-round access and close contact. Downtown specialty and department stores still serve a distinctive purpose, despite all the suburban branch activity. The main complaint that customers seem to have about the new suburban branch department stores is on the score of variety and completeness of stock, which of course depends largely on size. A downtown specialty or department store, because it has fuller stock, caters to the region as a whole.

So do certain government establishments and the main libraries and museums. These are actvities for which the economy of scale is so important that the whole region is best served from just one place. This will continue to be true as far ahead as one can see. There are activities that need a central location chiefly for the sake of a very flexible labor supply, dependent on mass transit. This is one of the reasons for style garment industries remaining in central business districts. In this and some other lines there is need for many business visitors, which calls for a location handy to intercity transport terminals. The implications of this factor change with development of various services for getting to and from airports. Other activities that remain central are small, new, and highly specialized businesses that depend on the wide range of contact advantages I mentioned before, including availability of rental factory space in old buildings, business services, forwarding agents, and so forth. This elaborate array of services generally exists in full bloom only in the very thick of things. So the central city acts characteristically as a nursery for new small enterprises and also a location for highly changeable fashion industries.

The upshot is that the locational status of the central city and the central business district is changing. The central areas are no longer good for some of their former functions, but possibly are better than before for some other functions (or could be made so).

Let me close with some thoughts about the adaptation to the changed situation. It has become obvious that the shift in central functions is not being made gracefully or even painlessly. Central business districts, and whole central cities, are problem areas nearly everywhere these days.

Why is the adjustment so difficult? For one thing, the central areas are the *oldest*. They are, not surprisingly, then, burdened the most by certain features of obsolescence of physical facilities if nothing else. They are the most heavily built up, in tons of buildings per acre. Any change of land use involving demolition or renovation is thus more costly there than anywhere else. The costs of real estate acquisition are very high. Property is parceled out in very small pieces, making it difficult to assemble parcels for any redevelopment. Difficulty arises, too, because some of the adjustments call for reduced intensity of use, and reduced coverage of land. The essence of the difficulty, really, is that we have adopted widely a form of passenger transportation that is too space-using to serve an area of concentrated contact, i.e., central business area.

There are some other reasons, of course, but less crucial ones. The outward movement of business and of upper- and middle-income population groups tends to shrink the tax base and helps put the municipality into fiscal difficulties. Unfortunately, also, the policies affecting transportation in particular have so far been at cross purposes; we haven't really figured out what it is we're trying to let into central areas or what functions we are trying to have them serve.

We need a view of what the central city is inherently fitted for. If its usefulness has declined in certain functions, perhaps we can find others where its usefulness, at least potentially, has increased. The central business district in New York, for instance, seems to have become increasingly attractive for central office functions. This may be a virtually unique case. But possibly central areas can specialize more as cultural centers. We may develop more largely, through redevelopment, a special kind of residence appealing to people generally without children, who like to live centrally. We need also some kind of way of assessing realistically the total economic and social cost involved in getting people in and out of central cities—treating automobile movement and parking and mass transit all as part of a single process, and trying to assess the costs where they really belong.

One objective that seems almost certainly wrong and perhaps catastrophically wasteful, is to try, as some people seem to argue we should, to make it eventually possible for ever-increasing numbers of people to travel to and in the central core exclusively in their own cars.

Comments by Edward E. Smuts

Economic and Urban Development Consultant
Pittsburgh, Pennsylvania

We have arrived at our present state of urban development as a result of the functioning of a variety of economic decisions and processes in addition to a variety of social, cultural, and physical considerations. As we observe our present state, we conclude that it is in so many ways inadequate, inefficient, and troublesome. One of our first responsibilities, if we are ever to achieve any betterment of our situation, is to evaluate how we have arrived at our present condition and to try to project where we might go from here based on a variety of assumptions, some of which are essentially of a status quo nature and others involving a high degree of intervention in order to redirect our development.

I suppose we could conclude even now that such analysis will almost certainly dictate a series of interventions in order to redirect our development toward goals as we now interpret them. This, in turn, raises the

16

very practical question of how we actually proceed to intervene in order to mold trends in favor of new goals.

Having mentioned goals, I now find it necessary to note a number of qualifications because I have serious doubts as to our ability to set intelligent and meaningful long-range goals in our present circumstances. First, I believe that as we improve our ability to evaluate economic, social, and political trends we will, at the same time, sharpen our ability to evaluate reasonably harmonious goals, i.e., goals in harmony with the life objectives of a significant segment of our population. Second, I believe we must design all of our physical developments with a maximum of flexibility to adjust for our errors in goal setting and evaluation of development trends and timing.

While I believe that we should make every effort to evaluate trends and to set goals and work toward them, the remarks which follow will be directed toward minimizing the cost of our errors in this worthy process. This emphasis should not be construed as inordinate pessimism as to our ability either to set goals or to guide and intervene in our future economic and social development. On the other hand, it is based on a realistic opinion of the practical inability of any combination of minds to anticipate all of the major developments which lie ahead or their specific timing.

In any forecast of future economic activity, there must be the implication that all assumptions will not materialize nor plans come to fruition. As we make economic forecasts and, in turn, translate these into the planning process and begin to arrive at physical decisions, whether they be for public or private facilities or whether they be conscious or merely reactive decisions, they, nevertheless, result in physical development which commits a particular area and a particular sum of money for a considerable period of time. It is my contention that the more we can provide a regulatory atmosphere and physical conditions conducive to physical adjustments as conditions and requirements change, without at the same time disturbing the practical value of the facility in terms of present needs, the more likely we are to minimize wasteful community or private expenditures on facilities with an early obsolescence factor. I would like to illustrate this concept with several examples.

Luther Gulick has made a considerable contribution to thinking with regard to community design by asserting that we should design activity areas with a certain ultimate capacity in the same manner that we design an office building or other structure with an elevator system and service facilities related to a given building pattern and maximum capacity. He notes that in an office building there is considerable latitude for different types of offices and office layouts. At the same time, there are certain ground rules as to the use of space which permit the building to remain efficient for a long period of time. Applying this thinking to a downtown area or to any other economic cluster such as a shopping center, industrial center, or residential subdivision, we see that increasingly we are providing for land use in large areas in which transportation, parking, property access, service facilities, and other functional elements are all given balanced attention, and once relationships have been fixed, controls are established to prevent any upset of the balance. Having argued for flexibility the foregoing observations may seem, at first, somewhat contradictory. However, since we cannot indulge in unlimited flexibility, it becomes essential to minimize as much as possible the need for adjustment by providing some ultimate capacity point and by clearly establishing the balance of facilities which will be required at this ultimate point. Thus, I feel we must first design to capacity within certain large areas or clusters of economic activity and then try to design in as much flexibility for long-range adjustment within this area. This parallels the situation of providing movable walls in a building to permit maximum flexibility of layout. In a downtown area this would take the form of providing for eventual demolition of certain structures as they become physically obsolete and their replacement with new, but similar, facilities.

Victor Gruen in his Fort Worth plan for the downtown area has also developed an example of the capacity concept in practice. It should be apparent that the adoption of concepts involved in the Fort Worth plan will be somewhat disruptive to the present patterns of downtown area development which rely on a consistent rise in the value of land and apparently steady increases in densities. It is my view that we must design our downtown areas so that at a certain saturation or capacity level, they will reach an optimum efficiency in the use of land for private functions as well as for transportation, parking, and other facilities. Once capacity level has been reached, any development of new capacity must take place outside the area. Within the area it is anticipated that continuous adjustments would be made but that the general character of use and capacity would not be adjusted.

As an example of the need to be able to anticipate certain capacities and types of activity in certain areas, we have the transportation study now underway in Allegheny County. As a key element of this study there will be a forecast of economic activities. The accommodation of these activities within the total area land supply will be considered and assumptions made as to the density of development likely to be permitted in various areas. Fortunately, provision is made for continuation of this study and for the revision of conclusions as improved economic data and indications of land-use controls become available. Even now, without benefit of firm capacity decisions having been made for such areas as the downtown, the study will be helpful in defining highway and mass transit network needs to accommodate existing development and allowing for expansion in certain areas to accommodate the ultimate projected development. It should be noted that one of the most crucial decisions required in this study is related to the division of passenger movements between mass transit and automobiles which is, in turn, related to many factors apart from physical development patterns in a direct sense.

It should be apparent that the better we are able to define capacity of functional areas or clusters within our metropolitan regions, the better will be our decisions on major public facility installations. This, in turn, implies controls which, to some, would appear severely to restrict private decision-making. On the contrary, I would maintain that by setting ground rules for general development patterns in specific areas and at the same time making commitments to provide certain public facilities to service those areas, we could actually then permit a large degree of freedom in the design and character of land use within the area. Furthermore, private investors in the area could be guaranteed a quality of development and services which it is now impossible to offer within an area under highly diversified ownership and without original controls. At the same time the community minimizes its facility investment and has long-term assurance of the adequacy of these facilities even though substantial adjustments may take place in the private facilities.

I believe this concept—of designing to a capacity and at the same time maintaining maximum flexibility— must be applied throughout our metropolitan regions. For example, I believe it must be applied to the so-called "gray area" between the downtown centers and the suburbs which Raymond Vernon and others have described as functionless and deteriorating areas draining the economic vitality of our metropolitan areas. Obviously, in some areas our ability to establish function and, in turn, capacity will be severely limited. Nevertheless, I believe we must make interim decisions in even the fuzziest cases because some form of development, even if only deterioration, is taking place in all sections of our metropolitan area. Actually, the real opportunity for intensive application of the capacity-and-flexibility concept lies first in the downtown core area. I believe that its application here may, in turn, give some guidance as to functions which might be introduced into the gray areas on a cluster basis. For example, many of our downtown areas are now the locus of unstandardized production or services by small enterprises involving a high degree of interrelationship with similar and allied enterprises. Because of other demands for downtown space, it may be possible to relocate whole clusters of activity into modern facilities in the so-called "gray area" thus releasing the downtown space for controlled use by office or other space demands.

Incidentally, I suppose I should make it clear that in speaking of controls on capacity and character of development, I am not referring to zoning as now conceived as the major control measure. In fact, I believe that much of our zoning unaccompanied by effective master planning has been the primary contributor to a reduction in flexibility and at the same time has resulted in a complete inability to stem the rise in density of activity in many areas far beyond the practical capacity of either existing or even modernized public facilities.

Also, I want to avoid giving the impression that I feel that any one individual or combination of individuals could determine the economic and physical destiny of a community in the sense of fully planned and controlled development. I do not propose that in controlling capacity of development we do anything which is actually more restrictive than our present controls. I do urge that we develop new types of control measures based on more thorough economic analysis and physical master planning involving close collaboration between private and public agencies. As applied to residential areas, for example, we might be much better off if we set a certain over-all density requirement and perhaps some access controls and then left it to the developer to arrive at a final design pattern which might mix single and multiple family dwelling units.

I believe that in order to move effectively and with reasonable speed into a situation in which we have more reasonable and practical control over the capacity of development we must generally increase the scale of our development projects. This means essentially more large-scale subdivision, more industrial districts, more shopping centers. It need not mean, however, the exclusion of the small builder who could operate just as well to build individual homes in a larger subdivision plan prepared by a major developer. But generally, I do believe that land development as such must increasingly be placed under the control of individuals, syndicates, or other combinations of ownership for the development stage with preservation-type controls provided after a development has been completed.

In general, then, I think it is important that we seek to improve our methods for arriving at community decisions regarding the character and capacity of development. Much of the challenge in developing improved techniques for arriving at better community decisions on development alternatives rests with professional planners. I hope an increasing number will see the challenge in this light and not in the narrow sense which I am afraid many of them do.

Comments by A. M. Woodruff

Dean, School of Government, The George Washington University

The growth patterns of metropolitan areas are closely associated with their internal transportation systems. The many American cities which grew rapidly during the era of the trolley car bear its unmistakable mark. The trolley reigned through the last third of the nineteenth century and the first third of the twentieth and influenced American urban geography to an extent that will take a generation of redevelopment to undo. To give but one example of growth in this era, Pittsburgh changed from a city of 86,076 in 1870, covering 23.1 square miles, to a metropolitan area of 1,953,668 in 1930, spread over 1,626.05 square miles.

The street car constituted the first big change in urban transportation since Abraham left Ur. Subway and elevated systems were merely elaborations of the same type of transit. Urban travel was made cheap and easy, but limited as to destination, and the starfish pattern of city growth resulted.

Trolley tracks were naturally laid on the principal avenues and led to *the* center. Before the trolley, every citizen could walk a short distance in any direction unless stopped by some barrier. The trolley expanded his orbit greatly but changed it from a small circle to a long ribbon with one end anchored downtown. All shoppers were within a short ride of the central city and the great department store was one of the resultant hallmarks of the age. The central part of the city was *the* one place everyone could reach easily, and land—both in the immediate center and on its fringes—rose to high levels of value.

As cities doubled and redoubled in size, the resultant street pattern reflected the transportation media and houses and other structures were located accordingly. Houses stand durably as monuments to conditions prevailing when they were built; thus, the downtown area of most "trolley car" cities is surrounded by a wide belt of structures fronting on streets well planned for an earlier age but an ingeniously effective barrier to easy access by automobile.

The auto began to displace the trolley in the nineteen-thirties, and the bus picked up only a fraction of the passengers formerly carried by street railway. Again the statistics for Pittsburgh are revealing and are reasonably typical of the older cities of the eastern part of the country. Thirty years ago the major street railway lines carried about 253,000,000 passengers, not counting some interurban traffic; in 1958, the number carried by both trolleys and busses was less than 1,000,000,000 in a metropolitan district which had grown substantially in population and much more so in area. In 1958, about 60 per cent of the former riders were either staying home or riding in private cars.

As autos superseded the trolley, a flexible medium of

transportation was superimposed on inhospitably rigid geography. In a sense, the type of urban movement represented by the auto is a throwback to earlier ages before the trolley car when urban populations walked and the choice of destination was subject to few limitations. The pattern of ancient and medieval cities is well known and, while they were more compact than their modern counterparts, urban facilities were more dispersed within them. These old cities, nevertheless, had downtown areas. Thus, there is no historical evidence that flexible forms of transportation lead to such dispersal as to suppress entirely the central part of the city. There is, in fact, considerable evidence to the contrary.

While the auto, like a man afoot, can go in any direction, unlike the man it requires a wide and unimpeded street. As mentioned above, in trolley car cities the access streets leading to downtown are frequently narrow, clogged with parked cars, and sometimes blocked entirely when something stalls a trolley. Measuring convenience against the wider selection, more and more shoppers have been turning their autos away from downtown. As a result, staggering sums of money now flow through suburban integrated shopping centers which offer easy access, parking, and a fair selection of merchandise.

The monopolistic accessibility of downtown during the trolley car era was reflected in high land values. The peak came in the late twenties when downtown land in several cities reached a ratio of about 600/1 compared with medium-grade side street house lots. Such scanty evidence as we have supports no such differential in pre-trolley communities. As the automobile began to dominate urban transportation and as the monopolistic position of downtown was more and more effectively challenged, the value ratio of downtown land to other land was much reduced. The automobile also reduced "close-in" residential land values, but the effect on downtown has been relatively greater. In 1958, in a number of cities of medium size, downtown values stood in a ratio of about 200/1 to residential land of about the same quality mentioned above. These ratios are far from precise, and vary from city to city, but indicate the trend.

Downtown, nevertheless, continues to provide the widest selection of goods and services in any city. Collectively it retains considerable economic muscle and political influence. Furthermore, it traditionally pours more tax money into the city coffers than it takes out in public services. Despite the astronomical cost, there have thus been good reasons behind the road building programs designed to break the bottlenecks and let automobiles approach downtown. Enough of them have been built to give some adumbration of results. Downtown land values seem to have stabilized in the inner core, although they are still crumbling at the fringes, and the downtown district probably still has a fairly firm long-term lease on economic life.

Chapter Two

The Evolving Metropolis and New Technology

by Richard L. Meier
School of Natural Resources, University of Michigan

Research and development presently serve as the greatest single source of change in the American society, and most of this change has repercussions in cities, since the population in the countryside beyond the commuting limit is rapidly thinning out. If we are to design and program the best possible future for metropolitan areas, we must take these changes into account.

A projection of the probable impact of new technology and new scientific ideas can only be accomplished by studying the trends in scientific fields, particularly applied science, and appraising the time that is required for exploiting these contributions. Fortunately many of the changes only provide better ways for doing what is being done now—the new activities demand little change in land use, circulation pattern, and the type of structure required.

The major changes anticipated stem from the revolu-

28

tion in communications which is likely to result in changes in modes of organization and in greatly improved coordination of services. We have yet to feel the full effects of the use of automobiles, for example. The consequences of these technologies for cities will be elaborated upon.

The principal conclusion is that the tools now used by planners for analyzing the potentials the future holds are valid over the ten to twenty-five year span. The study of technology and new developments in science need only be applied to certain crucial, rapidly-changing sectors. It will also be noted that there is no means of taking into account scientific discoveries which have not yet occurred, but fortunately there is a lag of ten to forty years in getting large-scale concrete applications of important ideas. Therefore it is unlikely they would be the cause of much premature obsolescence.

We shall use as our mode of discussion an outline of facts and trends in technological innovation having significance for metropolitan planning, with comments on recent developments and implications of special interest to planners and administrators.

Before the basic statements and comments are introduced some explanation must be made regarding the source of the information. It is compiled from a wide range of scientific and technical journals corroborated by discussions with investigators. The evaluation of the reports represents "a second order approximation" arrived at by techniques which were described in a recent publication ("The Social Consequences of Scientific Discovery," *American Journal of Physics* 25, 1957, pp. 602-13). The material was selected in the same fashion as might have occurred if the city planners had an intelligence system whose purpose was to discern movements in science and technology that could affect metropolitan development.

Automation

1. Automatic production plants in general have $100,000 or more invested per full-time job and are almost always multi-shift operations. Most so-called "automatic factories" retain some stages which require regular human intervention and therefore represent compromises with the principle.

An excellent article on this subject was recently published by Professor James R. Bright ("Does Automation Raise Skill Requirements?" *Harvard Business Review,* July, 1958). It cuts through a lot of the mish-mash that has recently been published on the organization of the newer forms of technology. He establishes the stages of mechanization and automation, their implications for skill of worker and degree of investment, and discusses the kind of industrial organization required.

2. The primary motivation for automation is seldom labor saving but most often the maintenance of quality of output under conditions of mass production. The interests in quality control will be reflected in strong demands for *dependability* of services and other inputs to the process, and this includes public services.

3. Automatic plants require much less floor space per unit of output (30-70 per cent). Since labor force is small, and spread over several shifts, an even greater reduction in needs for parking and circulation space is to be expected. For a given firm or category of production, automation requires greater emphasis upon high quality clerical and mechanical skills in the labor force.

4. Fully automatic plants tend to be prestige operations (engineering departments usually insist upon this) and therefore attention is paid to architecture and landscaping. Exceptions to this generalization are to be found primarily where the bulk of the output is under government contract.

5. The dependence of stable operations upon materials-flow to and from the plant means that site choice is highly dependent upon pipelines, waterfronts, mainline railroads, or trucking routes and upon airports for emergency maintenance. The demands are

so specific that planning can only be conducted on a plant by plant basis. A plan for an industrial estate for automatic factories, in general, is not likely to be feasible for a long time.

There is now, for instance, an attempt in Chicago to create an industrial estate for automatic factories. A computer, available on a rental basis, is to be located in the middle of the plot. It provides the locational incentive, supposedly, to fill eighty acres with high-grade industry. A glance at the cost accounting to be done in such firms, however, suggests that it is going to be very difficult, even in a large metropolitan area like Chicago, to fill an industrial estate with a multiplicity of small automatic factories.

6. Some of the most important automation will evolve in certain urban services, such as banking, insurance, security and commodity markets, printing, etc. These facilities are market-oriented, locating in a sixty to ninety minute ring removed from the major central business districts.

In the case of banking, some important developments have recently been reported from New York and Canada, but the Bank of America in California has made progress on the most massive scale. After six or seven years of development, ERMA has come into existence. ERMA is scheduled to take over in stages almost all the routine accounting operations for the Bank of America. Since this bank has hundreds of branches, regional centers will need to be selected for ERMA installations which serve twenty to sixty or so banks. The central headquarters for computation are likely to remain in the neighborhood of Stanford.

Decentralization of insurance activities is going on quite rapidly. Perhaps in another five years they will be at the stage that the Bank of America is now. In the instance of security and commodity markets, many engineers have had great fun designing substitute mechanisms. There has not been much interest on the part of

31

the officials (One reaction has been, "Where will we find jobs for Yale men in New York if such a monster comes into operation?). The first completely automatic commodity exchange was installed in 1957 in the Pacific Northwest. Plywood, hardboard, and other wood-based building materials were to be transferred from dealer to dealer and manufacturer to wholesaler by its agency. The enterprise went bankrupt within months because certain large suppliers refused to deal with a machine. It will be a useful datum to discover now who buys the equipment and what new kind of commodity exchange will be promoted.

The sixty to ninety minute ring attracts these activities because technical help is rather plentiful in outlying districts. There is less dependence upon female labor and, therefore, less attraction to the city center. The requirement also that there be landscaping fits in with suburban surroundings. Therefore, as the automation of clerical work proceeds, we may expect decentralization about that far out, but no further.

7. In the long run one expects a clustering of highly automatic units in the general vicinity of atomic power plants.

Atomic Power

1. The anticipated costs for electricity from nuclear fission reactors that have been published and widely quoted in the past few years have been excessively optimistic. Nevertheless, there seems to be justification for the installation of commercial plants of economic dimensions (hundreds of megawatts capacity) starting in the early 1960's.

The feeling now is that almost all the new plants in the world that are installed over the next seven years will be in Europe. After that time there may be enough cost-reducing experience to start on American plants in places like Minneapolis or the Pacific Northwest which are furthest from coal and natural gas.

32

Curiously enough there are no serious suggestions for large installations in New England. The reason for this is that the growth in demand for a given power supply area, or grid, must amount to several thousand kilowatts within three to four years before an economic size atomic power plant can be justified. This growth in demand is not anticipated for any metropolitan grid in New England, whereas areas with lesser population, but more rapid growth may get atomic plants.

2. The optimum sites are isolated points on peninsulas, islands, or other areas not suitable for urban development which are fifteen to fifty miles from the metropolitan center. Large volumes of cooling water are absolutely essential—more than any equivalent size plants use at this time. The prospective uses for radioactive wastes so far have trivial economic value and no locational effects.

3. Integrated complexes of electrochemical and electrometallurgical facilities are likely to evolve close to the power production sites because these locales provide service and byproduct facilities equal to the best that are expected to be available in the sixties and seventies. These complexes tend to be highly automatic—almost as much so as the nuclear reactor itself.

4. The developments in the effort to achieve fusion power using light elements intead of uranium are still not explicit enough to enter into metropolitan plans and projections. One or more crucial inventions are awaited. Only after these have been found and translated into technological proposals will there be a chance to appraise the impact upon metropolitan structure.

After the large-scale declassification of data on thermonuclear power experiments in Geneva during the summer of 1958, it became quite evident that "fusion" plants, if they are ever feasible at all, will have very close to the same locational requirements as the present nuclear reactors—except that thermonuclear facilities should be still larger and more complex. Thus we can imagine in the most distant future that the very largest and most rapidly growing metropolitan areas may get thermonuclear installations, while those the size of Pittsburgh, comprising only a few millions, must get along with ordinary fission reactors.

Electronics

1. The electronics industry is moving toward miniaturization and the automatic manufacture of components, as well as increased variety and complexity in the instruments and equipment it produces. Rates of obsolescence are more rapid than in any other industry.

2. Because transport costs are small, and the production process is modified so often, the smaller plants are "footloose." They can move to any spot with an easily trained labor supply. Assembly operations use a high proportion of female labor.

These factors inherent in the electronics industry are greatly changing the ideas of economists regarding optimal programs for economic development in poorer parts of the world. The older doctrine held that the developing area would have to start with textiles, shoes, and similar products; then, as they acquired skills, the industrial system would be ready for light metal fabrication, pottery, cement, and products of that sort; about a generation or so later they could move into the electronics age. Actually, it was found in Puerto Rico that labor productivity in the traditional industries reached 40-70 per cent of that in the United States in equivalent jobs, but in the footloose electronic plants, makers of components and subassemblies, the same workers could reach 100 per cent of American productivity. One finds that many places in the South (North Carolina, for example), have made comparable discoveries. It is possible now to jump from agricultural and the least mechanical of the local trades directly into the electronic age. The highly industrialized metropolitan area cannot beat this kind of competition, so it should attempt to attract only those activities associated with research and development operations.

34

3. Henceforth the location of the plants is likely to be divorced more and more from the research and development laboratories that gave them birth and the population centers that provided a suitable labor reserve to meet the peaks in production. Outer suburbs containing lower income families and small cities are very suitable locations.

4. The low levels of noise, dust, smoke, and fumes in these operations suggest that such plants do not need to be segregated too carefully from residential areas. However, due to the mobility of the industry, it may often leave the building to some successor operation which is less desirable.

Synthetic Chemicals
(including plastics, fibers, papers, rubber)

1. Despite considerable increases in output that are programmed, the level of employment is expected to remain constant for the nation as a whole. Within the industry, pharmaceuticals are expected to expand in both output and employment, and a new multibillion dollar "chemical fuel" industry for jet propulsion is likely to be created in the 1960's.

2. Chemical industries continue to cluster in complexes, based upon petroleum refining, natural gas pipelines, natural salt deposits, or hydroelectric power. In the future it is expected that new complexes based upon wood, agricultural products, coal, lignite, and atomic power will prosper and proliferate.

3. Many of the operations in an industrial chemical complex will constitute a threat to amenity. Air pollution, water pollution, and sometimes noise and truck traffic, are common but, when subjected to pressure, all of these can be controlled within reasonable limits.

Here we are saying something about the industry which has nothing to do with the technology, but the kinds of management these industries tend to have. Most managers have a highly technical training with degrees in engineering and science and are extremely public relations conscious. Their arms are easily twisted by any planner who understands these sensitivities. For example, it took only a minor threat on the part of the Mayor and the Los Angeles Planning Commission to bring about an investment of as much as a hundred million dollars in the prevention of the escape of hydrocarbon gases from refineries, oil fields, and bulk-plants in the Los Angeles basin, even though it could be demonstrated by laboratory experiments that the industrial contribution to smog was almost trivial as compared to the effects of automobile exhaust. The public relations leverage was such that these firms did far more than their share.

4. A fully grown complex of chemical industry may occupy several square miles of industrial land, therefore early provisions for expansion are crucial. Shift work, high pay, and the coincident small-sized car pools encourage disperse settlement patterns, much of it of a rural non-farm type.

Technicians earning $5,000-7,000 a year tend to commute from rural plots and small farms as much as thirty miles each way per day. Therefore, the parking lots must be larger than normal for multi-shift plants (i.e., the car pools are small or non-existent). An important part of the specialized horticultural production in a metropolitan area is likely to be connected with the spare time activities of such workers.

It should be pointed out in passing that plastics are going into construction very, very slowly. There are some claims, most recently in the British plastics industry, that a fifty fold increase is due involving many billions of pounds of plastics annually. I see absolutely no evidence for this scale of expansion, although the present developmental effort should bring about an expanding market.

Water Processing

1. The current programs aimed at the reduction of stream and shoreline pollution, combined with the special requirements placed upon water entering many manufacturing processes, are greatly increasing the amount of water being treated for re-use.

Nevertheless, the sums expended for this purpose are at best a few per cent of the investment in heavy water-using facilities, more often only a few tenths of a per cent. Most prospective pure water shortages can be removed through moderate expansions of such outlays.

A good friend of mine is consultant to the state of California on its water problems—among the solutions suggested is a proposal to transfer water from the Columbia River down to as far as Los Angeles. He finds himself the declared enemy of the engineers because he shows them that, by their own calculations, they could get pure water for the metropolitan regions at about one-tenth the cost by doing things that are not at all spectacular. In particular, they have avoided transferring irrigation water to the cities, although the crops that the water produces are surplus and must be sold at slashed prices or given away.

2. The gravest difficulties that can be foreseen have to do with the handling of radioactive contaminants (mainly due to the high standards which have been set from the beginning) and processing of oil shales and lignites in arid territories.

There is a hint that this prospect may now be changing. A thermonuclear explosion in a thick bed of shale may liquify the product economically, but it will be many years before we have adequate data.

3. The methods of de-salting sea water seem to be converging upon a cost level of about $100 per acre foot (30 cents per 1,000 gallons) for very large-size facilities at sea level. Pumping costs will add considerably to the delivered price. The techniques are expected to have minor applications over the next several decades, mainly in the treatment of brackish water at certain inland points where costs depending upon size of facilities, chemical constitution of the water, and byproduct values are brought down to more reasonable levels.

Food Processing

1. Increased processing of food stuffs (frozen mainly, but perhaps radiation-sterilized later), particularly leading to ready-to-

serve products, is to be expected. The best locations seem to be the outskirts of metropolitan areas or rural areas having a relatively dense population.

The key to this development is the acceptance of an "automatic kitchen"—an oven-like mechanism that uses ultra high radio frequency waves to cook things quickly from the inside out, infra red to cook from the outside in, and hot air for dehydration, all balanced for different portions on the plate according to a setting of dials. It has been designed, but the use cannot proceed until specialty restaurants and other food processors start producing ready-to-consume dishes in large enough volume to justify mass fabrication of the equipment. The circle of inhibitions will probably continue until the equipment is installed in the upper-class apartments due to be constructed in increasing numbers in the central areas of large cities. Any such reorganization of food production is likely to have repercussions in the rich agricultural belts that normally surround metropolitan areas.

2. It is quite possible, perhaps probable, that meat-packing complexes will decentralize, regrouping in the outlying points, and be based even more upon trucking than at present. The decline of the larger stockyard areas is already evident but the change is most likely to occur when a major producer encounters financial difficulties and is forced to retrench.

Defense Industries

1. During the 1960's the principal expenditures appear to be in the areas of missiles, precision electronic equipment, and chemical fuels for purposes of maintaining a stalemate in strategic weapons and roughly equal investments in a highly mobile force for coping with "brushfire" conflicts. Chemical fuels are necessary also for the exploration of space, an activity that is likely to become significant in the sixties and thereafter.

2. Centers responsible for military research and development are likely to maintain a continuing flow, however, of quick-developing manufacturing activities. The new plants set up elsewhere

are vulnerable to obsolescence in two to five years. For local planners, they should be considered as an opportunity to develop facilities suitable for occupation by a more stable industry at a later date.

The implications of military research for cities often border upon the fantastic. A new possibility has appeared on the scene in the past few months that is worth mentioning as an illustration.

The much-discussed newly discovered Van Allen radiation belts surround the earth except at the poles. Therefore if we wish to send animals or men safely into space it now appears that the launching sites must be close to the North or South poles. The final stages in rocket fuel manufacture are associated with the launching. Billions of dollars of expenditure are involved, so the choice of site would be made for technical reasons alone and not for amenities associated with the site. The design for a city in a spot like Antarctica would present novel problems, and we may expect some interesting technical innovations to arise from such developments.

Helicopters and Related Systems

1. The shortage of free airspace over metropolitan areas is expected to hold down the numbers of heliocopters operating. The possibilities of collision, particularly in bad weather, combined with the economics, force a movement toward helicopters with the passenger capacity of a bus.

2. The light portable types may serve many special purposes, especially in construction, but the chances of collision with structures is so great in cities that one expects their use to be strictly limited. It is impossible yet to appraise the utility and the costs of the vertical jet, "magic carpet" type of vehicle.

The chances of collision with structures in the city is being reduced with the development of "ducted fan" type vehicles. They can have bumpers around them that cushion shocks.

The claims of the manufacturers of VTO (vertical

take off) craft will be heard within two or three years. At least one design is intended to move into the commuter market. This should not be taken too seriously; for example, traffic engineers at the University of California showed that six to eight passenger vehicles coming from distances of fifty miles or so out could only handle about 10 per cent of the labor force before the sky over the plant would be saturated.

3. The major effects over the next two decades would appear to be the tying into the metropolitan region of certain points fifty to one hundred miles from the center. The exurbanites using helicopter commuter routes could move out a bit further along the rail lines and freeways that connect with the center.

4. If helicopter services must pay their own way and raise their own capital, a prospect which is now the likeliest of any, the rate of growth will be disappointingly slow.

The costs for the new metropolitan aircraft now run twenty-five to thirty cents per seat-mile, but with still more advanced equipment it may come down to ten to twelve cents per seat-mile. This should be compared with three cents per seat-mile on commercial inter-city aircraft and one to two cents per seat-mile for automobiles.

New Directions for Planners

1. In certain critical areas of information-gathering, such as traffic flow, unemployment statistics, accident rates, and air pollution, the data-processing is rapidly becoming more elaborate and more sophisticated. Programs will be developed shortly for handling much of this work on computers. The planning units would do well to exploit these new developments in order to find more lasting solutions to larger problems of urban growth.

2. Methods need to be found for collecting equivalent data for leisure time activities and preferences. Rates of change in this aspect of urban life are often very great so that much more detailed information is required than for the more stable aspects of life. Perhaps what is required is a continuous assessment of how people prefer to use their free time. Planners have far too many

other responsibilities to take the initiative in this direction, but they can reinforce the efforts of social scientists and market researchers.

One example here may be useful. The television industry is concerned about the fact that the average set-owning family used to spend fifty-six person hours per week looking at television and now this seems to have fallen below thirty hours. What were people doing with all that time before they had television? What are people doing with the time now that they are taking it back again? We may eventually get some basic data on recreational activities, the kind of information which permits us to determine where parks should be located and what kind of equipment to put into them, incidental to the worries of networks and major advertisers.

Recent research on state parks in California suggests that people behave as if their time in the park is worth about two dollars per person more than what they have paid in the way of incidental expenses—about eight or nine dollars per capita, as I recall. This kind of information is equally valuable for determining the limits to investment in recreation facilities.

3. New relationships between residence and place of employment must be thought out. Much of the new industrial activity segregates itself as a matter of choice, but a large share of the remainder might again be brought into close contact with residential and commercial land use.

4. Even before significant advances may be reasonably anticipated in the direction of metropolitan government the technology is fusing the metropolises together. We need several solutions to relatively continuous urbanism containing many differentiated foci of commercial, industrial, and recreational activity. Some formal solutions will probably derive from various types of functional studies; but the dramatic proposals that combine esthetic values with economic and political realism should come from planners.

It seems that it may take all of a generation to create

metropolitan government in America, and even longer than that in some metropolitan areas; and about that time I suspect that the concept of the metropolitan region, upon which it is based, will be obsolete. We are likely to find that altogether new forms of urbanism are becoming dominant. But these issues would form a sequel to the present presentation.

Comments by Thomas E. Stelson

Head, Department of Civil Engineering
Carnegie Institute of Technology

The information and conclusions presented by Dr. Meier are a fasinating glimpse into his crystal ball.

In the discussion of the projection of past and current trends into the future for planning purposes, I think of the mathematical term "extrapolation"—the projection of a function beyond known conditions. The extrapolation process often depends more on art rather than science and one thing that is certain about such operations is that many predictions that seem sound today will be wrong when the final situation is known.

In a broad view there are three elements that have a basic effect on long-range planning. One is energy, the second is materials, and the third is people. Since the first two are widely affected by technological development and change, evolving conditions will also be greatly dependent on changing technology.

The production, transmission, and economic avail-

43

ability of energy is a prime factor in the development of most modern industries and cities. Present studies indicate that energy sources like atomic fission and fusion will ultimately, if not rather rapidly, be replaced by solar energy. Such technological change will have a tremendous impact on municipal location and development. Popular residential areas in sunny locations such as Florida and California will have distinct economic advantage over cloudy districts such as Pittsburgh where economic development has been primarily stimulated by the availability of carbon fuel.

The second aspect, that of materials, is probably even more important in long-range planning. New materials and new concepts about the utilization of old materials are developing at a fantastic pace. In basic construction, for example, structural steel, wood, and concrete were the only materials used in the past. Now there are dozens of common basic structural materials—alloys of aluminum, alloys of steel, wood and plastic laminates, and plastics. All have special areas where they can be economically justified. By themselves most of these specialty items are not used in significant quantities but as a total they are very significant and becoming more important each year.

New materials and new methods of using materials provide imaginative resources for engineers and architects that were unavailable in the past. Furthermore, new ideas, such as those coming from solid state physics studies may lead to unheard of and undreamed of developments. For example, filament strengths of one million pounds per square inch have been measured in the same materials that now have a design strength of twenty thousand pounds per square inch—a fifty fold increase. If such knowledge can be utilized, all construction and design would be drastically changed.

The third and final item, that of people, is the most fascinating, I think, because it is the least predictable. For example, the best minds in the automotive industry were delighted when families decided that they preferred two cars rather than one car. Projected demands on this basis were unduly optimistic because families decided they did not want four cars instead of two cars. This is typical of mistakes that have been and will continue to be made. The television statistics given by Dr. Meier must also indicate some sort of unpredicted transition in the television industry.

The ultimate effect upon a metropolis of such advances in the technology of energy and material will, I believe, cause decentralization to some extent. Common functions that affect urban areas, like flood control, water supply, sewerage disposal, electric power, and heating fuel will be of less economic advantage in specific regions. With refinement in technology, transportation systems will eliminate much of the local economical advantage, just as natural gas is now piped from the southwest to New England and most other places in the country.

With decentralization, the demand on transportation systems will be increased and transportation problems will become a greater headache than they are now.

Planning, I think, will become even more fascinating in the future with greater mobility, easier transportation, new and better materials, cheaper and more abundant energy. Change will be more rapid and the success or mistakes of planning will be more rapidly revealed.

Chapter Three

The Culture and Esthetics of the Urban Community

by Norman Rice

Dean, College of Fine Arts, Carnegie Institute of Technology

First, let us define what we have been asked to consider: The culture of the urban community and the esthetics of the urban community.

The culture is clearly the resultant of all the forces working within the metropolitan complex. It is something we share, in greater or less degree, wherever we are—in cities or away from them, through such culture-compelling devices as magazines, radio, television, cinema, reproductions, recordings, machine duplication, and billboards. But it is surely in the cities that our culture is most sharply defined, most deliberately culti-vated. We have lost some of our sensitivity to the charge laid against us by many a visiting European that we are a nation of borrowed culture or no culture at all. If we take Matthew Arnold's definition of culture as "acquaintance with the best that has been known and said in the world" it can fairly be said that we are doing

46

our best to bring that acquaintance into being. We are building fine symphonies, fine art galleries, fine libraries, fine universities. These shape one aspect of urban culture and the cities share, take pride in, reflect whatever glories emanate from their great cultural institutions. This is one face of urban culture; the other is its opposite, and is less appealing.

Cities and governments more often benefit from than take responsibility for their great cultural achievements. There are few places in this country where music and theater and painting and dance are considered by populations, and thus governments, to be respectable outlets for tax money. An overpass or an arena can more easily attract tax support than a theater or gallery. The contribution of the city of Chicago to its Art Institute was for many years (I don't know how things are now) just enough to keep up with the annual building maintenance costs. It is, to be sure, no longer immoral to buy books with public money (though someone else, more often than not, puts up the library building), but it is wrong to buy pictures, or support an opera, or subsidize a theater. These activities in our culture are traditionally the responsibility of wealthy individuals and not of the public in general.

All this is not surprising, particularly considering the nature of our education. Here I can do no better than quote from Robert Ulich's book *Conditions of Civilized Living:*

It is partly due to the utilitarian (though essentially highly unpractical) trend in education, and partly to the influx of culturally unprepared people into positions of educational importance that we lay at the present so extremely little value on a more systematic esthetic education. One can be professor at a great university and profess without shame his complete indifference to anything that belongs to art, rhythm, and beauty. Yet, in our oldest document on education, Plato's *Republic,* there is

47

clearly emphasized the necessity of building all special instruction on a broad esthetic, or as he calls it, "musical" education. By this he means a form of schooling which (through the medium of dance and the singing of sacred hymns) conveys to the young a sense for the harmony of soul and body.

The typical modern education is one-sidedly rationalistic, with the effect that it achieves little even in the realm of the intellect; for the intellect has to be nourished by emotional impulses in order to be productive. Of the potential influence which music and rhythmical education can have on the formation and harmonization of a personality, most of our educators have no idea. But at the same time they deplore that the increase of school and the lengthening of school age has failed to have a sufficiently beneficent effect on our civilization. As if this great product of the human race, namely spiritual culture, could be achieved if more and more young people for more and more time become exposed to teachers and professors who themselves have "souls without music."

That other aspect of the culture of cities which Lewis Mumford discusses, takes as its definition of culture a more extended view (from *The Culture of Cities*):

The city, as one finds it in history, is the point of a maximum concentration for the power and culture of a community. It is the place where the diffused rays of many separate beams of life fall into focus, with gains in both social effectiveness and significance. The city is the form and symbol of an integrated social relationship: it is the seat of the temple, the market, the hall of justice, the academy of learning. Here in the city the goods of civilization are multiplied and manifolded; here is where human experience is transformed into viable signs, symbols, patterns of conduct, systems of order. Here is where the issues of civilization are focused: here, too, ritual passes on occasion into the active drama of a fully differentiated and self-conscious society.

Thus the culture of the urban community is at once the expression of a broad range of activities—amorphous, diffuse, dynamic, shaping, blending—in short reflective of the many states of mind that are contained within the city's orbit. Also, it is that sharpened, particularized element which represents the best the city is able to present of itself at any moment in history: an aspect which is the product of its most thoughtful, imaginative, cultured, and creative citizens. This aspect—which, incidently, brings culture and esthetics into fusion—has been well described by Mumford:

> Cities are a product of time. They are the molds in which men's lifetimes have cooled and congealed, giving lasting shape, by way of art, to moments that would otherwise vanish with the living and leave no means of renewal or wider participation behind them. In the city, time becomes visible: buildings and monuments and public ways, more open than the written record, more subject to the gaze of many men than the scattered artifacts of the countryside, leave an imprint upon the minds even of the ignorant or the indifferent.... Layer upon layer, past times preserve themselves in the city until life itself is finally threatened with suffocation: then, in sheer defense, modern man invents the museum.
>
> The city is a fact in nature, like a cave, a run of mackerel or an ant-heap. But it is also a conscious work of art, and it holds within its communal framework many simpler and more personal forms of art. Mind takes form in the city; and in turn, urban forms condition mind. For space, no less than time, is artfully reorganized in cities: in boundary lines and silhouettes, in the fixing of horizontal planes and vertical peaks, in utilizing or denying the natural site, the city records the attitude of a culture and an epoch to the fundamental facts of its existence. The dome and the spire, the open avenue and the closed court, tell the story, not merely of different physical accommodations, but of essentially different conceptions of man's destiny. The city is both a physical utility for collective living and a symbol of those collective purposes and unanimities that arise under such favoring circumstance. With language itself, it remains man's greatest work of art.

But what of esthetics specifically?

Esthetics is a philosophical discipline through which judgments are brought to bear on any of the works of man, including cities. It is the philosophy of taste, or the perception of the beautiful. It is, in short, the way we explain our reactions to things which in themselves

49

are without utilitarian or rational moment, but which, in the long history of man, may be our most enduring monument. That cities have been frizzled on the esthetic frying pan, by Frank Lloyd Wright and others, is a commonplace of comment. But that men honestly aspire to beauty in their cities is no less true, and the esthetic experience is one which legitimately belongs to the urban dweller no less than do the bucolic pleasures which we associate with nature to those who choose to inhabit the country.

The esthetics of the urban community would appear to be at once active and passive, including both the quality of judgment the designers can bring to bear on the problems of the cities and the resultant response (and thus presumably the heightened pleasure) that cities which provide esthetic experience can provide for their citizens.

Architects, I am afraid, are at once the ones best qualified to establish esthetic values in our cities, and the ones most responsible for their lack. I hasten to add that these two circumstances are rarely brought about by the *same* architects. But architects are not the only ones involved in esthetic judgments, nor are they always the ones who can bring about the best conditions they seek. Cities, if they are anything, are a great bundle of compromises, some of which have worked out very well and some badly. If you want examples I can give them, but you can see for yourselves what happens to a good idea right here in Pittsburgh when it is confronted by the strategy of business or government.

By examining the esthetic experiences which derive from the urban scene we can perhaps attain some insight into the ways in which an urban environment can sharpen the city dweller's esthetic perceptions, and increase the delight a human being deserves as compensation for the inevitable drawbacks of city living. Anyone who takes delight in cities can make a list. But here is one from my own experience:

To begin with, the city as a mass can have proportion —or only size. The awareness of mass and scale is most apparent in the great port cities, where the distant view, as in Naples or New York or San Francisco reveals the city as a monumental, mysterious structure, promising excitement, visually compelling, dramatic and filled with life. The approach to the plains cities, as oases among broad bands of corn and wheat is sometimes no less compelling. And the miracle of lights as the traveler comes into a great city by night—by plane or ship —is sufficient transformation to achieve for even the dreariest city a momentary glamor—usually dispelled promptly by the realities of port or air terminal.

Movement is another city characteristic which can have true esthetic appeal. Movement of light, whether formally organized or not—movement of color and shapes in vehicles and people—movement quite consciously contrived, as in the Rockefeller City skating rink, or movement accidentally realized, as in the transitions from light to dark as one moves across the store-front façades, encountering light, shadow, softness, sharpness and the shift of a thousand forms, reflecting, asserting, sedately poised or shimmering, along with such cheerful accents as man has been able to add—a bright color on the buses, a few pots of flowers, the crisp heraldic pattern of a flag. These city events can be part of esthetic experience and I think many people consider them so without assigning them so pretentious a name. Nature helps cities, too, when it snows or rains, or when the bright sky gives emphasis to a high structure.

The cities most favored are the ones which can evoke a sense of nature without too much artificiality or pretense. The lake front in Chicago is an unforgettable part of my life and I have spent many hours in fascinated consideration of all the qualities which give it its unique character—the breakwaters, boulders, yacht harbors, beaches and promenades, its threatening and benign moods, its night mystery and its incessant but appealing sounds. Also, who in San Francisco can ever forget the sea? How wise are the city builders who value such attributes as wharves and beaches and boat basins and make them a cogent part of urban experience. Rivers have values, too, which too frequently are submerged by other considerations. The bridges in Pittsburgh, though they could be much better, are still a fine sight, and so are the barges and smaller craft that bring to the rivers a life and movement which on some occasions (and on more if we could see the rivers from afoot with greater ease) give back deep esthetic pleasure to the passing citizen.

The configuration of architectural units is so obvious and so conscious an esthetic element that one can add little to what you must already know. Of course no city is uniformly fortunate in its architecture. New York has its Seagram building and its Rockefeller City, but it also has its awkward Ziggurats. Chicago's lakefront absurdities, vintage 1920, are no pleasure in themselves. They are at their esthetic best when their architectural elements are obscured by night or the elements and only their orderly layering of lights, or dimly perceived proportions remain.

I have talked about the masses of cities, the alliance of cities with nature, the pleasures of movement both as a participant on the urban scene and as a spectator (what a wonderful idea is a sidewalk café when conditions are right), the qualities of mass illumination and color which belong characteristically to cities, and the esthetic worth of individual structures to the whole. I haven't mentioned parks, which are really rural interludes, or other more formally planned rest spaces within a city complex. These have their esthetic values, of course, but they are no better than nature can contrive without cities and are generally better understood as esthetic attributes, and therefore better managed, than some other city-generated sights and sounds I have mentioned.

There should be some discussion too, of elevations, both natural (as in San Francisco or Pittsburgh or Edinburgh) and man made (as in the Eiffel Tower and the skyscrapers of Manhattan). These can contribute to man's sense of the city's scale, serving both as foci and as platforms from which the structure of the city, and thus its ordering, can be apprehended and viewed with fresh delight.

But against all these things (and many more) which can, I think, legitimately be ranged on the side of esthetic experience and at the same time are inherently urban, can be placed the anti-esthetic experiences of city life, which not only can nullify so much that is admirable, but can actually destroy the esthetic gains which planners and designers have worked to achieve. You can make this list yourselves, too. But I must mention the smells, the offensive litter, the squalor, the inconsiderate small acts, the tangle of impatient traffic, the carbon monoxide delays, the near view of so many badly conceived structures, the disorder of lights confusing warnings with merchandising, the out-of-control advertising, the grimy little corners and the great slums, which seem to be part of the heritage of cities and which never quite are coped with in effective and permanent ways. The most heartening counteraction against these city blights comes from such projects as the self-help neighborhood renewal programs in Philadelphia and

53

elsewhere. But this is a slow and painful business. It needs to gain in scope and intensity if it is to make a real difference to many people in many places.

What can planning do about all this? I would think that it could insist on positive esthetic solutions—that is, design solutions—to *every* problem it considers. Just a political or a sociological solution, without supporting physical assertion of the ideas of civic order, control and rich visual and participation experience, is hardly enough. The esthetic reaction is in *people* not in things. But things can evoke the experience; conditions can permit the esthetic reaction to emerge (or can stifle it). The *designer* is the key to growth of esthetic judgment.

Behind every esthetically successful city program there has been some one, or a group, possessed of highly geared discrimination. The Acropolis was no accident, nor was the Chicago lake front park, nor were the great boulevards of Paris, the carefully wrought squares of Florence, the bridges of Venice, the prewar baroque splendors of Dresden and Munich. When a city has reached a point at which the reaction of its own citizens is one of corporate admiration for the sights and sounds of daily experience, if it is a city which the traveler discovers with pleasure and returns to as often as he can, if it generates in recollection a sense of being aware of itself and proud of its urban status, then I think it may be said to have developed cultural identity. If at the same time there is in it a preponderance of things which give visual pleasure, which urge participation in its urban life, which are ennobling rather than degrading to the senses, then it has the capacity to give esthetic satisfaction as well. There are few such cities. But we can always hope.

Comments by Walter Read Hovey

Head, Henry Clay Frick Fine Arts Department, University of Pittsburgh

One has only to look about to realize that in spite of the many blunders and lapses of taste in our present program for improving the city we have reason to hope for the kind of environment envisaged by Dean Rice. I would like to add a few comments to what Dean Rice has already said.

In the history of design one finds that floral ornament, such as the beautiful decorative art of Alexandria, is fostered in crowded areas. I suppose there is a nostalgia on the part of city people for the open fields and they tend to poetize those things, like flowers which are connected with the country. But I doubt if the park is, as Dean Rice suggested, a bit of country in the city, a rural interlude. For a park is usually a formal thing, even involving the sophistication of mathematical theory. It is a matter of using Nature in a way that would never have been thought of in the country. It may be created purely for esthetic effect or it may be a setting for numerous interests and activities as well as a place of escape. The formal garden is known to us principally through the great seventeenth century achievements, such as Versailles. It evolved out of the principles of design found in the architecture of the high renaissance in Italy and later elaborated in the designing of cities. It was not strange then that the garden design of Versailles should have been used for the plan of the city of Washington made by Major L'Enfant.

Today there is a great problem in keeping people—or at least certain groups of them—within the city. Surely it is a matter of developing a participation in the life of the city so that the city-dweller feels that he belongs there and wants to belong there and does not want to stray away. The city must not only be interesting but beautiful to accomplish this and the problem is a vital one for the planner.

S. Gièdion in a recent book, *Architecture, You and Me,* writes of the importance of what he calls the "core of the city." He emphasizes that here is where meeting places should exist in accordance with the special interests of many groups. The social backgrounds of cities vary considerably and attention must be given to the kinds of things that are of particular interest to the various groups involved. It is a mistake to create again for one city a design that developed in another city, perhaps in another generation and in another society. Even though it were a very impressive design, if it did not evolve as a part of the life of that particular locale, I doubt if it would ever really stimulate pride in the city or make people want to belong to that environment.

It is important that the city planner think of suitable gathering places for entertainments, festivals and events related to local interests. And such places should vary in scale and setting. The expression, "furnishings of the city," has been used to describe the accessories such as fountains and sculpture which add distinction and stimulate pride in a community. One thinks of the excellent use made of the Spanish steps in Rome when they are banked with flowers, stalls along the banks of the Seine in Paris, or out-of-door art exhibits on the Boston Commons. Cities, too, often have vantage points for beautiful views which are overlooked. When this sort of environment is developed, the desire is aroused to participate in city activities and to begrudge the time spent in retreating to the monotonous suburbs.

It is coming to be realized that the city support of cultural enterprises is a good investment as it keeps people within the city limits whose taxes form a considerable loss when they move to a suburban district. The support of the city of Pittsburgh for the Arts and Crafts Center is a recognition of this fact. Here the important thing is that support is given to an activity rather than to a collection of objects. Libraries have long had public support (and museums occasionally receive public funds), whereas such support for contemporary expression in music or the other arts is extremely rare. Yet it is the contemporary symbol which gives vitality to a community. It is the constant expression of an emotional response in terms of the changing times, which under the spell of art, keep the forces of destruction from taking command.

Three stages in the city plan have been defined as representing three distinct values which have been dominant in American society; the commercial stage which resulted in the gridiron plan, the engineer's approach which touched especially the problems of traffic and sanitation, and finally the "intellectual" approach which begins to realize the importance of the city as an esthetic

57

expression. The town planner might well be thought of as the greatest of all artists for his problems are the most comprehensive.

If the American city is to survive it must be made beautiful. If the United States is to maintain its position as a world power it must reflect its leadership in its own society. The beautiful city is a well organized city. The issues are of the greatest importance and today is the great moment of challenge.

Chapter Four

Sociological Research and Urban Planning

by Donald J. Bogue
Professor of Sociology, University of Chicago

Good planning is based on facts and verified principles, but facts and principles can be had only as the end-product of research. Therefore, good planning that improves upon *laissez faire* must be preceded by good research.

But doing good research is itself a specialty. Although there are many research tasks the planner can do for himself, there are many fundamental ones he cannot handle because they are too complex and specialized. For example, modern research is cheaper and faster than the old-fashioned planning surveys because it makes use of modern methods of sampling coupled with modern methods of making statistical inferences from samples. Few planners are equipped to design an efficient sample, put it into effect in the field, and handle it properly in the tabulation and analysis stage. Similar complexities and technical specialties might be cited for "depth interviewing" to obtain information about human wants and needs and other aspects of research. Few planners can spend the time and energy necessary to become research specialists. Moreover, the task of planning is so huge that it is beyond their limits of time and energy to do all of the research and all of the planning, too. Instead, *the planner must become a highly enlightened consumer of other people's research, and learn to be a close collaborator with researchers.*

Therefore, it is my opinion and strong recommendation that if the two institutions (University of Pittsburgh and Carnegie Institute of Technology) launch a program to train planners, one of the cornerstones of that program must be a respect for, an application of, and training in the use of research reports and in collaborative planning of research studies.

To this point I have talked about "research" generally. I'm sure most people will agree that what I have said makes sense when applied to planning traffic systems, shopping centers, and razing substandard housing, for here research on traffic flows, trading areas, and conditions of buildings is a most obvious need. But, you might ask, what does sociology have to contribute by way of research that would be useful in planning?

In my opinion, there are at least five major branches of sociological analysis that can contribute to the basic need to "get the facts and understand the situation" and to "find out what action would be most appropriate." They are:

Population studies—the study of the size, distribution, and composition of urban and metropolitan populations—and changes in these aspects, for the particular area being planned.

Human ecology—the study of the community as an economic and social organization of patterned relationships—spatial, temporal, and functional—with particular emphasis upon livelihood activities (labor force, occupations, industries, etc.).

Social organization—the study of the human groupings in the community: memberships, participation in community institutions, the institutions themselves, and the "customs," "habits," and "values" of the residents for which planning is to be done.

Social disorganization and community problems—the study of social conditions that are regarded as problematic or pathological. Many planners overlook the fact that planning areas are problem areas, and many of the people living there are problem people.

Social Psychology—the study of individuals as members and participants of groups within the urban community, and of their attitudes and opinions—and how these are formed and changed.

If people are researched from these five angles (or the combination of angles that the particular problem deserves) I believe the planner then can have a firm footing upon which to build his plans. Therefore, I would like to summarize, *very briefly,* what kinds of research can be performed in each of these areas that can be useful as a foundation for good planning.

Population Studies. These can be broken down into three sub-fields.

1. Study of the number of inhabitants, and the growth of these numbers. This includes studies of fertility, mortality, migration.

2. Study of population composition, including: how many families in an area, the ages, sex, race, occupation, income, educational level, and marital status of the population.

3. Study of changes and trends in population, including: analysis, interpretation, and explanation.

In the past demographers have been interested in problems on the national level. As urban planning has come to be more important, the demographers have been concerning themselves with local problems.

When a planner goes to work on a locality the first information that he desires concerns the population. How many people and families, what are the age groupings, what is the ethnic composition, the income levels, the occupations, and the educational level of the inhabitants. He wants to know how the area is changing, he wants descriptions and explanations for the changes. In response to the need for this kind of information on the local level, the Census Bureau has added census tracts for individual city blocks in the next census. Planners need this information about small areas because in planning they often deal with relatively small and limited areas. Planners may find that information by city block may not be what they require, and may need information concerning one face of a city block in some cases.

Human Ecology

The human ecologist views the city as being in important degree a livelihood mechanism, as a means for earning a living. The planner must realize that a city must be functional as well as livable. The ecologist reminds the planner that the city is an economic unit.

The ecologist draws maps to show how things are distributed in space, e.g., factories, schools, stores, etc. Ecologists will show how low standard housing and delinquency rates in a city are related. In recent times they have attempted to become less descriptive and to develop principles and theories of ecology, e.g., prediction of racial population shifts within a city, or explanation of transportation behavior in terms of business activity.

Social Organization

Some sociologists and planning people (those with a rural bias) have damned the city for its hard, impersonal, and formal human relationships, in contrast with the warm friendly relationships of country areas. These people have tried to convince the planners that there is no hope for the city. Current research by sociologists have shown that these things are not true, that there are informal groups and warmth in personal relationships in the city. The sociologist has a vast area of unresearched material in regard to the city. The planner can use information supplied by the sociologist in planning for livable cities.

Social Disorganization

Every community has problem situations. The city tends to act like a giant sorting machine in that it tends to sort like people out and deposit them in the same areas. The poor tend to live in little pockets, alcoholics concentrate in the skid-rows. Many pockets present problems, some do not. The planner is usually concerned with solving problems in the problem pockets. Within a problem pocket there is often a great deal of social disorganization; however, planners often feel that the people they are dealing with are just average Americans who have had the bad luck of living in substandard housing. This is not true. Many of these people are faced with serious problems, e.g., alcoholism on the part of the family head, disabling injury to the breadwinner. The planner is often faced with a sample of problems among human beings which he just does not comprehend. The skid-row problem is being completely avoided in current redevelopment programs. No one knows what to do with the skid-rows. If they are torn down, will a number of little skid-rows pop up in other parts of the city? The planner actually doesn't know what kind of people are living on skid-row, and what it is he can do for them. This is just the area in which social research can provide the planner with accurate information regarding the people he is planning for.

Planning and the Urban Community

Social Psychology

Planners often tend to deny the value of social psychological and attitude research and claim that it has no place in planning. They say that if you ask someone how he would like it if such and such a thing were done, he can't really tell you because you are asking him to experience something he's never experienced; e.g., you can't ask people how they would like to live in high-rise apartment buildings if they've never tried to raise children in such apartments. In spite of this criticism there are some situations where social psychology has a definite place in planning. The first of these is in a suggestion box type of question. If you are going to plan the redevelopment of an area and have the same people living there afterwards, you should ask them what it is about the area that they do not like. People may not be as disturbed over the physical buildings as much as they are over street disturbances, muggings, purse-snatchings, etc.; they may want something done about crime in the area. They may feel that shopping facilities are adequate, but street lighting or smoke elimination may need to be improved. The second area in which the social psychologist may be of help is in regard to prejudice.

A planner may make the mistake of assuming that the people he is planning for understand the problems of the area and will go along with the programs he designs. All too often this fails to be the case. People have prejudices, tastes, and biases and they just do not behave the way the planner thought they would and do not act in accordance with the plan. The social psychologist can go into an area and find out the tastes and prejudices of the people, so the planner can either plan with them in mind or undertake a program of education designed to minimize the prejudices and prepare the people for the plan.

The appreciation of the problems in planning from a sociological point of view will enable the planner to take a much wider perspective. He will realize that taking the skid-row alcoholic out of the flophouse and placing him in good low-cost housing is not going to solve his problems. Physical planning is not enough. Planning must be human and include the welfare department, juvenile officers, family court workers, and other city agencies. This is being recognized more and more in city planning organizations. The role of the sociologist is to provide research for the broadened scope of planning.

Chapter Five

A Note on "Community"

by Perry L. Norton
Planning Consultant, Lexington, Massachusetts

The meaning of "community" is one of the basic unresolved questions confronting society and planning today. In the absence of a thorough understanding of community and in the absence of a modern dynamic *meaning* of community, we are building a physical living environment in which the individual is losing his identity. He is losing his capacity to communicate in a democratic way his personal desires and his response to the great social issues which affect his daily life and the legacy he leaves for his children.

In these notes I will attempt to show that our failure as planners and social scientists to deal imaginatively and vigorously with the problem of defining "community" has created a vacuum in which there has persisted an image of community at serious variance with the realities of today's complex industrial society. I will suggest that our cultural response to the fracturing of community form which has accompanied the urbanization process is the "nutrient" whence come our current metropolitan problems.

With the advent of the industrial revolution, the great migratory movements from Europe to this continent, and the world-wide population explosion, we have been propelled, abruptly, into a society which has completely disrupted the established community of the pre-industrial era. Where once people stayed put, now we move. Where once a man's "station in life" was usually decreed from birth, now we have wholly different patterns of class structure and elite groups. Where once we had an integrated man in an integrated society, now we have a man fractioned into several communities in a society where the interrelationships of these communities are constantly shifting.

It is important to note first that through many centuries there developed, as an essential characteristic of community, a polity of *communication* by which the identity and the performance of the individual in his several roles held substance. If he was a farmer, a tradesman, a blacksmith, a fisherman, or whatever, there was little doubt as to the accepted performance of his role. His other roles as a husband and father were equally clear, both in terms of the duties prescribed and the manner in which the duties were carried out.

The community itself was the purveyor of values—the self image of performance underwritten by a system of communication developed to a fine degree of effectiveness through centuries of experience. Many terms have been employed to describe this community: the established community; a society of meaningful face-to-face contacts; a community of belonging; etc.

The central question facing us is this: *can* we redefine

67

the individuality in terms of the physical community? This impinges, obviously, upon how we choose to define community. If we attempt to reconstruct community in the same general terms of the older era, I would suggest that we will fail in our service to the individual. If, on the other hand, we can establish an image of community more consonant with the realities of the day, then we have an opportunity to regain an effective role for the individual—and this, I submit, should be the main purpose of planning.

Unfortunately our efforts have not been in this latter direction. Our reaction to urbanization, and all that this implies, has been to deny the realities and to seek out *parts* of the whole on which to focus identity. In the planning field, for example, we have attempted to transfer the meaning of community from the old village system to the contemporary neighborhood. In some cities we have even used the word "community," which in our lexicon is a collection of physically related neighborhoods. Other efforts have led us into experiments such as "new towns" and "utopias," or into mathematical exercises on "optimum sized cities."

We have not been so completely naive as to think that in the neighborhood a man may find his full personality come to life, but we have tended to assume a kind of mystical aura of participation attaching itself thereto so that through this neighborhood, or "community," we believe that the individual is provided with an opportunity to become, once again, an effective member of his society.

Obviously planners are not alone in this. It is a re-action endemic to society as a whole. Witness, for example, the continuing isolation of the suburban parts of the metropolitan whole, the insistence upon non-involvement with the fantastic social issues confronting the central or core city. Witness the skill with which we have succeeded in positioning ourselves such that we are increasingly unable to solve metropolitan problems democratically, but have rather set into motion a system of authorities over whose principles of action we have little or no control.

Another kind of reaction is one of eternal busy-ness: clubs, associations, organizations, and institutions of incredible variety spring up to accommodate fractions of the total personality and in the doing compete for resources in a relentless manner leaving the individual exhausted, albeit rather sophisticated in his capacity to organize. Professional, fraternal, and social groups all claim wide orientation, but at best merely chip away at pieces in an uncoordinated fashion. This is almost inevitable and for two reasons: first, they are either organized on the basis of a highly specialized interest which will survive for survivals' sake; or, second, they have a limited geographical identification which, in the pursuit of "good neighborhoodship," would have them supporting the isolation of the part from the whole.

These reactions, which are lively and forceful, suggest that there exists a rather desperate striving for identity and that people turn, or are persuasively led, to those places where they feel they can make an impact. In the area surrounding the home place there is quite an array of such establishments ranging from local elective positions in the government to the PTA's and the Leagues of Women Voters. (This choice of examples is not strictly random, since it is quite obvious that these local roles are more often filled by women than by men.)

Now in many vital respects these are important activities and it should not be interpreted that they exist merely to sop up time. But it cannot be denied that they often become champions of "our town first" and

69

thereby contribute to the delinquency of our society to meet head on the forces which affect the shape and content of our living environment.

Others, as we have already suggested, search for identity in terms of specialized interests—often associated with work situations. By their very nature they often develop these specialties to a high degree and at the expense of other needs and problems. True it is that they "deal" with problems. True also that they conceptualize these problems in a comprehensive vertical framework. They *are* concerned with the relationship of the local interest group to regional, state, and national interests and concerns. But the focus remains on the specific problem or issue and there is no point in this vertical scale where one problem is related to another in terms of their joint impact upon the whole of society and the whole of the individual.

Let us look quickly at some of these problems and issues recalling, as we do, what has been posited thus far.

We start with a very rapidly increasing population. Forecasters are saying that in 1980 the population of the United States will reach 272 million. By the year 2000 it could pass the 350 million mark. Further, it is already observed that 85 per cent or more of new growth (as it is reflected in terms of the demand for housing, schools, highways, etc.) occurs in the urbanized portions of our country.

The fact is dramatically highlighted by the plans for the federal highway program. Six thousand of the forty-one thousand miles of the Interstate Highway system will be *urban* highways. The potentialities of this will be especially meaningful to any who have observed how land-use patterns are affected by the creation of new highways in urban areas. The appetite for land on or easily accessible to new routes is voracious. Traditional land-use patterns are challenged and all manner of competition for choice location ensues.

The highway people scramble for the land they need, often in secrecy and virtually never in the light of public debate (how *can* they do otherwise when the debate is necessarily on the basis of a piece by piece struggle with one town after another, each prepared to recognize the need for a highway but preferring that it be located next door?). And just as the highway people are concerned about the acquisition of adequate land for their purposes, so are all other interests which require land-space for their fulfillment.

Conservationists worry about the mass destruction of watersheds and the pollution of lakes and streams. They observe with some accuracy that careless building, uncontrolled building, so disrupts the natural course of water flow that excessive costs are incurred to correct the mistakes if, indeed, they can be corrected at all. Some "extremists" are already saying that it is no longer a question of simply changing policy from here forward, but that a reversal is required if we are to spare future generations subsistence at minimum levels.

The producers of food for the burgeoning populations are alarmed by the conversion to urban land uses of our Class-I farmlands. In California they are experimenting with agricultural classifications in urban zoning ordinances. Already, we are told, the cost of beef has begun an upward climb which is over and beyond any general inflation. The reason? The cattle-fattening lands of southern Illinois and eastern Pennsylvania are losing out in the short-range economic battle of competing land uses. And in the fringes of our metropolitan areas it is a common, and almost daily, observation to see truck farms and orchards give way to the gigantic

71

earth-moving equipment of the mass subdivision building industry.

Recreation specialists try to dramatize the incongruity of more and more leisure time and less and less space in which to enjoy it. Riparian rights to our streams and beaches is becoming a concept of antiquity. Reservations for game; forest preserves for outdoor sports; park land for just plain relaxation—are these mere platitudes? Have they any meaning, any value? Apparently not, judging from the agonizing difficulty the body politic has in deciding to hold land free from speculative development.

It is the thesis here that the difficulty stems from the absence of an image of community bearing a comprehensive relationship to total needs of society and the individual. It is seldom, for example, even within the planning field, that these macro-conflicts in land use are accepted as within the purview of urban planning—this in a society which is acknowledgedly urban.

But the micro-conflicts of the urban region are equally striking—and equally untouched. In the urban region, for example, the state highway department may be firming up plans for a major new highway, or extensive widening of an existing route. At the same time, a suburban community—through which parts of this highway will pass—may be purchasing a school site, or permitting the construction of new houses, or extending its utility system—and all of these directly on the planned-for right of way.

Another example: neighboring cities in the same urban region compete with one another to entice the owners of a "nice clean electronics plant" to locate within their borders so that the "winner" may look forward to a balanced tax base.

In the central portions of an urban region we are

clearing and rebuilding substantial parts of the city. We demolish slums and build luxury high-rise apartments because we feel it important somehow to reverse the trend of the migration of "leadership" from the city to the suburb. In the doing we ignore the fact that the total community is also lost to this "leadership" by our continued insistence that this, like the "tax base," is a matter of competition. And in the doing we also tend to neglect the embarrassing problem of relocation, thus forcing the creation of still more slums.

And so it goes, through the occasion of passing opportunity, that we build and rebuild our physical living environment, without any assurance that what we do stems from any organizing principle that will provide for an integrated human being who can function well and productively in a changing world.

The problem of community is so central in its positive and negative aspects to planning for our cities that this might well be the place where planners and social scientists could focus their joint intellectual efforts. What new content is appropriate to the idea of community in a mobile, urban, industrial society? To what extent can manipulation of urban space add to or detract from the content? What are the implications of a new concept of community for the form of a city? For the esthetics of a city? Where does the new concept make room for the individual? Where have the old ideas of community led city planning; and where have they led it astray?

There is certainly no simple answer to these questions. And this, perhaps, must be our first caveat. It is all too easy for us, as planners, to take up our pastels and superimpose new kidney-shaped forms upon a topographic map. It is all too easy for our society to avoid the larger issues and to deal daily with the squeakiest irritants. Yet we can no longer face casually the inescapable fact that we have lost a democratic communication and that we seem to be determined that it stay lost behind geographical and functional barriers.

In a free and democratic society, planners cannot and should not dictate what the "community" *shall* be. They can create an image of what happens in its absence and of what might happen in its presence. "Community" must start with communication through a recognition of common concern. It may be centuries yet before there can emerge a new physical form which is expressive of this communication. In the meantime we have the responsibility for observing and commenting upon the consequences of daily events affecting our environment.

It may be that the most lasting contribution of the planning movement will be its role as a forum of communication and its vibrations as a sounding board of change. It may well be that in planning we can begin the long and arduous task of creating an image of the larger community in which the factors of common interest in relation to locality are effectively coordinated with those of functional concern already establishing vertical lines of communication.

Unless we work in this arena, unless we "run scared" to fill this coordinative and integrative function, planning along with other urban-oriented disciplines will be left administering to a series of haphazard problem situations void of intellectual content.

Part Two

Metropolitan Politics and Organization for Planning

Metropolitan Politics and Organization for Planning

Most city planning is done by or for governmental bodies. It is evident, then, that its purpose and effectiveness will be closely tied to the manner in which it is organized within government—both formally (i.e., as it might be described on an organization chart) and informally (by way of politics and its relations with private groups and the public generally). This section of the volume examines the implications of various forms of organizing planning activities.

But one can say something about organizing an activity only after he has decided what is the nature of the activity he is organizing; and here the controversy over what is—and even more, what should be—the essential nature of urban planning comes strongly to the forefront. This controversy is carried over into Part Three, where a characterization of the nature of planning is an essential starting point for discussion of the planning

77

profession and of planning education. Not surprisingly, the question of just what is city planning emerges as the central controversy within the field at the present time.

In the Foreword to this volume, it was suggested that urban planning is going through the disorientation and the search for direction which is typical of a late-adolescent stage of development (seemingly of a field, as well as of persons). It is useful, in trying to understand the different views expressed in the volume as to the activities which should be central to city planning, to appreciate the fact the authors of the various papers are addressing themselves to different stages in the development of the planning field. That is, some of the authors are referring to what they think is particularly significant in present planning practice, while others address themselves to the question of what planning may or should become. To appreciate what is involved, it is suggestive to look at the development of the planning field, in terms of its past, present, and possible future foci.

It is useful in this regard to divide the development of the field into three periods, more or less covering three parts of the twentieth century: (1) from the turn of the century to about 1933 (while no single date can adequately mark a new period in the development of the field, 1933 is, of course, an unusually meaningful date for planning); (2) from the early thirties to some time in the sixties—that is, the current period; and (3) the remainder of the twentieth century. The designation of this long period into the future is meaningful, since students trained today can be expected to continue practicing to the end of the century before they retire.

The first period can be characterized as follows: A substantive focus on the *physical layout of the com-*

munity, with planning activities centering on the preparation of a mapped master plan and on zoning; activities carried out through an independent planning commission, a geographical-jurisdictional focus on the *municipality.* And the beginnings of an interest in economic, social, political aspects as they influence the three-dimensional city.

The second—or current—period can be said to have these features (generalizing very greatly, of course): A substantive focus on *urban development* and *redevelopment,* with planning activities centering on changing land use and the dynamic elements of project building and rebuilding, transportation flows, zoning changes, and so forth; the commission form of organization still dominant, but increasing ties of planning agencies to municipal executives; the *metropolis* as the main area of geographic-jurisdiction interest (accompanied by a sense of frustration because of the actual political scatteration); beginnings of an interest and some activity (such as long-range capital budgeting) in executive staff planning; also beginnings of an interest in the urban region (in the consequences of "megalopolis"), in planning for nonphysical elements, and in basic ideas underlying all planning—including decision-making.

The question for the future is: are any or all of these matters, in which a strong interest is developing, to become a substantive focus for planning activities? Should urban planning encompass executive staff planning (in close tie with other administrative staff functions such as budgeting) as well as over-all physical planning? If there is a central staff planning function, should it be just as much concerned with socio-economic matters as with physical matters (e.g., economic development, welfare service taken as a whole, youth and recreation services, "social adjustment" programs, and the like)? If urban governments are to be concerned with the planning of all these activities, then there may be at least four or even five "centers" of planning within the governmental structure. Thus, it is possible to conceive of urban planning in the larger urban communities as organized somewhat along the lines shown in the chart on page 81.

What this could add up to, then, are some five types of planning: (1) staff or "management" planning—charged with the planning of policy, and the charting of general goals to give direction to program and project plans developed at the departmental levels, (2) comprehensive physical planning, (3) general socio-economic planning, including what might be called "social welfare" or "human services" planning (which cuts across agency lines), (4) functional, or program, planning for various public services such as police, education, and public health, and (5) "project" planning, as in connection with housing and renewal activities, highways, and so forth. Many activities involve both functional and project planning. These various kinds of planning could be related to each other in many ways, and conceivably might be staffed entirely by generalist planners, by specialist planners, or by a mixture of the two. Given this unfolding future and all the possibilities that lie ahead, it is little wonder that the form that urban planning should take is a subject for lively controversy.

All this is made even more difficult by the fact that there is a large area of disagreement centering on the question of what form *metropolitan* planning should take, and, in fact whether what we need is metropolitan planning or a new kind of broad regional planning, given the very rapid development of urban regions

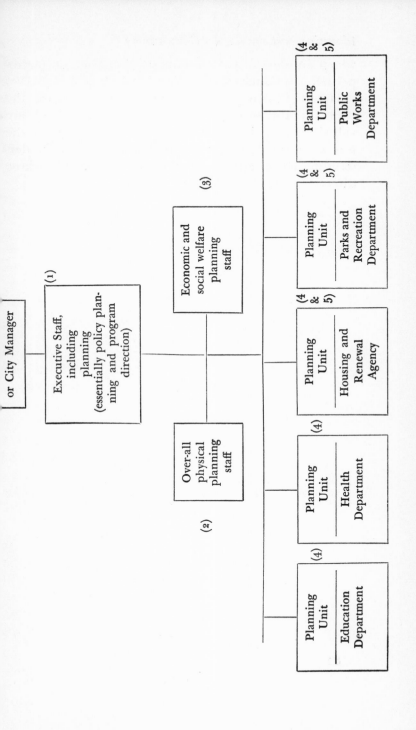

or City Manager

Executive Staff, including planning (essentially policy planning and program direction) (1)

Over-all physical planning staff (2)

Economic and social welfare planning staff (3)

Planning Unit / Education Department (4)

Planning Unit / Health Department (4)

Planning Unit / Housing and Renewal Agency (4 & 5)

Planning Unit / Parks and Recreation Department (4 & 5)

Planning Unit / Public Works Department (4 & 5)

which in some cases encompass a number of metropolitan communities.

However, seen in terms of an unfolding future, the papers in this section, and in Part Three as well, are valuable precisely because they bring the issues to the fore and provide materials which are helpful in understanding the alternatives for a professional field whose direction is far from firmly set.

Chapter Six

The Politics of the Metropolis

by Frederick Gutheim

President, Washington Center for Metropolitan Studies
Washington, D.C.

Planning is of interest to politicians as it influences voting; as it changes the established power structure in executive departments; as it alters the value of land; as it affects taxes and tax rates; as it causes the migration of substantial numbers of people; and as it offers evidence of success or failure in governmental stewardship. Other considerations might be mentioned, but these are sufficient to introduce the subject of the relationship of politics to planning.

Planning must be considered in relation to cities, to metropolitan regions, to larger areas defined by river basins or natural resources. It should also be recognized that planning for central business districts, for suburban communities, for industrial areas, or for transportation, urban redevelopment, housing, or other special purposes—each will present its own special aspects and interests. All, however, must have some relationship to the future, and to intelligent foresight into the future, if we are to consider them planning. And for the purposes of this paper, we should be concerned with comprehensive, multi-purpose planning rather than with more limited programs.

Henry Adams observed that practical politics consists in ignoring the facts. It may consist in more or less successful endeavors to conceal the facts, or to make them appear to mean something else, but I think it is impossible today for practical politics to ignore the facts. Further, it appears to me that more and more politicians are interested in the future, and are willing to put political bets on it, as distinguished from a more short-sighted and immediate concern with the next election, or tomorrow's vote. I might also risk the observation that while politicians are closely attuned to the immediate interests and concerns of their constituents, and reflect these in what they say and do, they are less likely to be fooled into thinking this is the whole story. For one thing, they often hear both sides of the story; for another, they know there will be a day of reckoning. These are some reasons for the growing sympathetic relationship between politics and planning.

Planners, too, are more interested in politics. Having worked for politicians most of my life, I believe I can say this was not always so. Planners used to think of themselves as designers, makers of plans, creators of the city beautiful. They were employed by city planning commissions organized deliberately in order to set them apart from the presumably corrupting influences of city hall. Their plans often graced the wall, or filled the filing cabinet, but—despite notable exceptions, such as Burnham's Chicago plan—frequently failed to be carried out. These experiences grew to stigmatize the entire planning profession. (Robert Walker, *The Planning*

Function in Urban Government, was the best critic.) They were notably responsible for the almost universal scrapping of planning work at the beginning of the Great Depression—at the very moment when, because of the work relief and public works programs, planning was most needed.

Planners swung the other way. They embraced that awful word "effectuation" with unabashed enthusiasm; they even set up jobs in planning offices for "effectuators." The acid test of a plan was whether it was executed; the criterion of professional success whether a planner "got results." Even politics received the pragmatic definition, "the art of the possible." There was a corresponding and deplorable neglect of those worthy inheritances from the profession of architecture: good drawing, models, careful presentation, well-written and printed reports. Instead, we were adrift in a world of mimeographed and badly written reports, a gush of technical language, public relations, and pseudo-public relations. From this period, I think we are now emerging. There is still a desire to appear practical, but generally planners are sufficiently secure, are now paid enough, and have a strong enough position in the power structure to be more relaxed and more willing to be concerned with their proper job.

The planner in a governmental structure today is well aware of how he can contribute to that work. He has such tools as the capital budget, the master plan of public works, the mandatory review, with which to exercise his influence over current work; and he has increasingly the techniques of public reporting and public relations with which to develop "a third force" of independent political strength based on the facts and on independent professional judgment. In his relation to legislative bodies, to city councils, the planner has also developed a

85

surprising strength. Where he has established what might be termed a consultative relation to such bodies, he has contributed enormously to grounding political "electricity" by relating specific controversial projects to more comprehensive and long-range factors. Where the issues have been closely drawn—and they frequently are —consideration in this broader frame of reference is frequently decisive.

Planners are working for politicians. They are not politicians themselves. This distinction is fundamental because we should not train planners to be politicians, much as they should be trained to understand politics and politicians; and we should not expect planners to be organized as parts of the political process, since their work is more related to that of the executive departments of cities, states, and the national administration.

John M. Gaus, in his Harvard report, *The Education of Planners,* strikes a very nice balance in dealing with this issue. Gaus maintained that planners should be trained to understand general administration and, especially, such staff services as the budgetary work of government where planning might be expected to make its principal contribution. He suggested that some planners might be educated whose main qualifications might not be in one of the "plan-making" fields such as architecture, landscape design, or engineering. His conclusion, substantially that later reached in Great Britain in the Schuster report, was that the ultimate leadership of a diversified planning team might fall to a planner trained mainly in physical planning or it might not, but that all required skills would have to have some common intellectual preparation, a broad area of mutual understanding, and also a common professional discipline.

One consequence of this philosophy of planning education as it was practiced at Harvard under the administration of G. Holmes Perkins was a subtantial increase in the richness of planning studies and school programs. The Harvard "new towns" studies were distinguished mainly by their realism from an economic and governmental point of view. Under Dean Sert this appears to have been lost, and whether the gains in design offset this loss is a moot point. Harvard illustrates better than any other school the struggle to give design its proper place in the planning curriculum. It also offers one of the best opportunities to train planners side by side with architects and landscape designers, to set collaborative design problems, and to encourage a mutual understanding and interdependence which is the foundation for later practice. But has such teamwork actually been realized? It is not my impression that it has. This does not invalidate the theory which Gaus enunciated, and to which Dean Sert gives at least nominal support today. It simply means more hard work must be done before it has meaning in planning education and practice.

My own interest in planning in recent years has been principally in metropolitan regional planning. In this work there is seldom any clear-cut administrative context such as city planning ordinarily has. And the political issues are both more lively and more confused. If the lack of specific responsibility for land use or other kinds of planning administration tend to diminish some political pressures, the greater breadth of planning and its concern with such factors as population migration, industrial dispersal, interregional highway programs, and the organization of state or federal programs on a metropolitan area basis give the regional planner a more bracing professional climate in which to operate. Most of the city planners, like Paul Opperman, who have moved over from city to metropolitan planning find it a stimulating experience for this reason. In the metropolitan scene, many planners find the "real problems" as defined by the social and economic realities of the metropolitan community, not the abstracted and fragmented problems with which a central city or suburban fragments must deal. Not the least stimulating part of this challenge is the need to create new political forms to deal with metropolitan education, metropolitan health, water, and sewage problems, transportation, and the rest of what might be called the metropolitan agenda. Here the planner joins forces with the political scientist and public administrator in the search for new forms of government.

Among the questions worth discussing in this context is whether it is possible or desirable to undertake metropolitan planning without creating first some framework of metropolitan government. I feel that experience strongly argues that much metropolitan planning can be done prior to the creation of any specific metropolitan government with powers. (I was unsuccessful several years ago in persuading the city of Philadelphia and the Pennsylvania Institute of State and Local Government that this was the case; but perhaps they feel differently now that they have had their premature try in Harrisburg to get metropolitan powers for the city of Philadelphia.) Indeed, metropolitan planning will help to develop an awareness of the need for such governmental structure and to specify more exactly what powers it should have and how it should be related to the other layers of government. Plunging directly into the creation of metropolitan government may even lead, if successful at all, to the neglect of the most promising roles of such new governmental forms. This seems to have been the experience in Toronto, and perhaps in metropolitan Miami. By contrast, and without regard to the racial implications of that decision, the creation of the

88

metropolitan consolidation of Nashville and Davidson County was strongly helped by the work of the planning agency.

It may be assumed, I think, that the metropolitan region has certain characteristic political interests and problems. It is with these that metropolitan planning must deal. I might identify them most readily as the problems of the central city, of the suburban periphery, and of the metropolitan region as an integrated whole.

In the central city the problems arising from metropolitan growth and expansion are those of *congestion,* as a limited central area must accommodate more and more activities; *of change,* as industry and much retailing leave for the suburbs and office building activities and more specialized trading find places in the city; and of the *movement of people and goods,* including mass transportation, expressways, and parking.

In the suburban areas, the problems arise chiefly as the result of growth, and typically are those of a *shortage of governmental services;* the *need for orderly planning* and scheduling of new activties and facilities; and *overcoming the political fragmentation* and arbitrary character of highly specialized residential or industrial communities, and the financial, racial, and other difficulties this imposes.

The metropolitan community as a whole can be dealt with only when some means are found for dealing with its governmental problems. Some of the customary ways this can be done (without regard to their political feasibility) are (1) annexation; (2) the creation of functional authorities; (3) the creation of multi-purpose or general metropolitan authorities; (4) city-county consolidation; and (5) the borough plan of metropolitan government. Short of some form of metropolitan government, progress can be made by various forms of private or public

89

efforts to survey the metropolitan community or to engage in metropolitan regional planning.

Since the monumental study directed by Coleman Woodbury, published five years ago, we have been wary of looking at the superficial evidences of slums and blighted areas as being of themselves metropolitan problems. Instead, we suppose they are evidences of racial migration, industrial location and change, organizational defects, and other underlying factors. This line of thinking is being deepened and broadened by the contemporary group of studies by ACTION, not least by that by Professors Banfield and Grodzins just published. This unconventional argument contends that metropolitan government itself is a reactionary movement.

Yet we must remember that it is with symptoms that people and their political leaders are concerned. Slums and bad housing, poor residential neighborhoods, are where it hurts most. We may be able to persuade them that the proper treatment is of the underlying malady, but I think we can ignore symptoms only at the peril of forfeiting the patient's confidence and faith in our understanding of his difficulty. If our remedies for metropolitan difficulties are to be acceptable, we will have to make sure that they affect the symptoms. And that they do not produce worse symptoms! The cure for downtown congestion is not a deserted city. The remedy for slums in the central city is not embryonic slums in the suburbs. Short-run highway solutions may lead only to worse difficulties.

Even the briefest treatment of this subject cannot neglect to mention the interest of the federal government in metropolitan planning. Initially, and most obviously, this derives from the fact that Title VII of the Housing Act of 1954, amended, provides the main grants in aid for metropolitan planning—poorly as these have been handled. More fundamentally, it arises from the fact that so many federal programs have as their end result the location of post offices or federal buildings in cities; the approval of federally aided programs of roads, airports, hospitals, housing, or urban redevelopment; the impact of federal policies of the regulation of transportation, communication of trade; the underwriting of such urban enterprises as housing.

The federal investment in the metropolitan areas of the United States today is probably well over twenty-five billion dollars. And there is no federal policy for cities and metropolitan areas, no effort to coordinate or direct these federal programs and interests in ways that contribute to the betterment of cities. Examples are abundant of federal agencies that ignore local planning. The policy of the Eisenhower administration, and of the Bureau of the Budget, is to ignore these issues or to pretend that some form of improved federal-state relations may ultimately improve them. The one effort of the Bureau of the Budget to establish a regional office with the avowed purpose of exploring what could be done to coordinate the short-sighted and narrow programs of federal bureaus was abandoned. Under the present circumstances, the federal relations to cities and metropolitan areas are not innocuously negative; they are positively divisive and disturbing. Even individual agencies and their programs are hopelessly enmeshed with metropolitan interests as, for example, civil defense. A survey of this situation, what it means, and what should be done about it, deserves a high place on the Congressional agenda.

Let me conclude these rather brief comments by some observations on the planning process itself. Please do not think that my interest in the plan as such and in design problems means that I am unaware of the process theory of decision-making. On the contrary, it is because I believe the plan as a design has an authority of its own that it becomes a powerful factor in the planning process. You have an excellent illustration of that in Pittsburgh where the Golden Triangle project exercised an influence upon much broader planning long before it was ever realized. The same force operates in plans of a larger significance than this limited measure of redevelopment. So long as a plan represents a valid set of facts and principles; so long as it is accepted as a political agreement; so long as it is an expression of popular determination—it must be reckoned with in the decision-making process. When it loses that authority it is finished as a plan. This conception of planning is one reason I am seldom much concerned with the legal status, or lack of it, of much metropolitan planning. Once you get over the money hurdle, the measure of planning's effectiveness is pretty directly related to how good the plans are rather than to the political strength that enforces them. I think it is easiest to see planning in this sense as comparable to organization or to budgeting—a set of influential guide lines rather than an inflexible document. We can reorganize, change the budget, or change the plan—but only where there is a good reason for doing it. This idea is horrifying to architects, engineers, or other people who look at planning as a kind of contract which, once it is accepted, is not to be changed because it has become the organizing instrument for work.

If we have plans, or perhaps you would prefer to call them planning policies, they also become the subject of political debate. Mayor Lee found this out in New Haven. Candidates were recently running for office in Miami with different conceptions of metropolitan government as their platforms. Cities are now beginning to find themselves in a trading position with suburban communities in the state legislatures.

To sum up, then, metropolitan planning must deal with the political issues of metropolitan growth and expansion and it must find political ways of getting its plans into action—whether these are short of the creation of some form of metropolitan government or actually propose such forms of government. If it deals with anything less than the whole range of metropolitan interests, it will cease to be accepted as metropolitan planning and become something else, as has been the case with private metropolitan planning efforts in Chicago, New York, and some other cities. And at that stage it is neither planning nor politics.

Comments by James W. Knox

Controller, Allegheny County, Pennsylvania

Contrary to popular belief, comprehensive planning today is not primarily aimed at making decisions for the far distant future. Basically, planning offers the best guide and chronologically-arranged outline of actions and services that must be provided to satisfy the most critical needs first, and then, that these fit harmoniously into the entire area development plan projected as far ahead as practicable. The plain but stubborn fact is that the wants of man are infinite while the resources available to satisfy them have specific limits. It is only through realistic planning that these wants can be satisfied by scheduling them in accordance with an equitable timetable.

The present metropolitan economy is spreading out more evenly over the metropolitan area, generating more traffic and bringing into focus the need for adequate highways, traffic control, parking and transit facilities together with the need for air and stream purity controls, environmental sanitation programs—the disposition of community sewage and wastes, etc. Cities, outlying regions, and rural areas are running into each other because housing developments, highways, shopping centers, recreational areas, etc. are reaching out farther and farther with little regard to existing municipal boundaries. Central cities and outlying areas are becoming more closely intertwined and it is becoming increasingly difficult to make a sharp distinction between the wants and problems of the city and those of the suburb.

All municipalities are concerned with their internal sovereign interests, the traditional preservation of home rule and autonomy being held sacred, so to furnish a specific public service on a regional basis is not an easy task.

The creation and adoption of the municipal authority is becoming increasingly popular. A certain degree of cooperation and resultant projects or services have been accomplished through the use of authorities but, at best, these legal mechanisms, fragmented and unrelated, have not adequately met the needs of metropolitan areas. *I believe there is a dire need for a central power or agency to act on specific problems and solve them by planning for the entire area. There is also a need for such an agency to assist in coordinating the various activities, to maintain a continuous "look" at the problem as it affects the whole area, and to promote an atmosphere of cooperation among the municipalities within the area.*

In Allegheny County the legal authority to create and effectively implement such an area agency lies within the control of the State General Assembly. Pennsylvania's state legislature is dominated by representatives from rural counties and the smaller units of government, who, in many instances, do not, as yet, feel the full impact of the problems of the city and suburb—be it Pittsburgh, Philadelphia, or any other area comparable in size, population, or activity. Consequently, since the state legislators write the law, the influence of this group is reflected in the legislation enacted by the restrictive amendments and by changes to the original bills to such an extent as to render them almost useless or ineffective.

As an elected county official, I am cognizant of these imposed limitations in the county code which define the scope and area of my administration as county controller. Again, as member of the Allegheny County Planning Commission (an arm of the Board of County Commissioners by their appointment), I feel the effects of these restrictive tendencies which were summoned by these same influences.

Members of the Board of County Commissioners are the administrators of highest rank in the county, but counties, as such, are creatures of the state, deriving all power therefrom and, consequently the commissioners, too, are subject to these same influences and resultant limitations.

Of course, I am quite aware, as I'm sure most of you are, of the potency of this issue as a political weapon in an election campaign and it is not confined to either side—the Democrats or Republicans. I well remember that one of the basic steps that had to be taken in Allegheny County and in Pittsburgh to start some real activity in planning and progress in this city, was the adoption of a legal ordinance by the city of Pittsburgh for the control of air pollution and specifically to eliminate smoke. And here, I might say, is one place where an elected official really put his political future on the block. I recall being present at some of the caucuses, meetings, and conferences that were held by the members of the Democratic Party and the very strong position assumed by the Mayor of Pittsburgh in support of smoke control and the proposed Smoke Control Ordinance. In the primary campaign, a member of his own party, then a member of City Council, announced as a candidate for mayor against him. At that time, there was no issue of high taxes, wage taxes, or city progress. The issue was SMOKE CONTROL. This opponent had adequate financing and spoke in behalf of the "little Joe's," living in the heart of the bituminous coal industry, who would be compelled to pay more for processed coal and so forth. Well do I remember how hard we had to work to save the Mayor's candidacy. His opponent received 65,000 votes and came within 20,000 votes of achieving victory. That was a great issue, and I think it is probably the most important single thing that has happened in our area to start us on the way to real planning and real progress.

Then there is the question of costs. That is always important and the perennial question is: Where do we get the money? Of course the only source is from taxes and again the control lies within the legislature. That body, through their controls, practically restricts the amount of money that may be appropriated for such programs. Sometimes it restricts the tax base to such an extent that real progress just cannot be achieved. The rural influences again are felt.

The fight on whether or not we're going to have a regional government has also generated a lot of political steam. It was an important issue in the last campaign and was used effectively to scare voters in the boroughs and townships into believing they were going to lose control of their own affairs. Being a good issue, it was used, not only by members of the Republican Party, but by many members of the Democratic Party as well

97

because they control a great number of local govern-ments. It is very difficult to try to talk a man out of an office, and that is what it amounts to when he feels that any talk about metropolitanism will cause loss of his job. Interestingly, too, the most coveted jobs are those that do not pay any salary. I think it's just the pride and the honor of holding the position. I can sum up my own views on this question briefly: We have some real prob-lems facing us in this great metropolitan area, but it is my firm belief we shall continue to enjoy a great deal of success without the need for abolishing the local municipal boundaries.

Comments by J. Steele Gow, Jr.

Staff Director, Regional Commission on Interrelationships of Secondary Schools, Colleges and Professional Schools University of Pittsburgh

I must take issue with Mr. Gutheim on the question "whether it is possible or desirable to undertake metropolitan planning without creating first some framework of metropolitan government." He says that "experience strongly argues that much metropolitan planning can be done prior to the creation of any specific metropolitan government with powers" and that "indeed, metropolitan planning will help to develop an awareness of the need for such governmental structure. . . ."

I agree that such planning can be done and perhaps is being done, but I doubt that metropolitan planning can have beneficial results if it is done in the absence of a metropolitan government.

The plans produced by metropolitan planning cannot be implemented by the many separate governmental units within the metropolitan area without a good deal more coordination than those units are likely to achieve

99

by voluntary cooperation. The planning is bound to highlight particular area-wide problems or needs, however, and the inclination then will be to establish *ad hoc* authorities to handle those particular problems or satisfy those particular needs. This will contribute to the further fragmentation of governmental units to confuse and befuddle the citizens in a metropolitan area. Already, in Pennsylvania's metropolitan areas, we have overdone this business of creating special purpose authorities and have badly splintered governmental powers. Because we find it easier to set up special authorities than to reorganize general government, we solve particular problems by complicating the big problem of coordinating government in the metropolitan community.

I doubt also that metropolitan planning will help develop awareness of the need for metropolitan government. In the first place, assigning particular functions to special authorities vitiates the public motivation to reorganize general government. The big problems are removed from the field of general government. And the prospects are dimmed for unscrambling these special authorities if a comprehensive metropolitan government is attempted.

In the second place, metropolitan planning without a metropolitan government probably means planning by some privately financed and controlled agency. Such metropolitan planning as we have had in this Pittsburgh area has been done by private agencies, by the Allegheny Conference on Community Development or its Regional Planning Association affiliate and perhaps by the Pennsylvania Economy League's Western Division. These organiaztions have done good work and served the community well. I criticize not them but the community which fails to provide a governmental agency to perform what is essentially a governmental service, that is to say planning, and so makes the community dependent on privately financed and controlled agencies.

Whether what these private agencies do is really metropolitan planning I will not attempt to say. But it is the nearest thing to metropolitan planning we have had here. And the result of it, as I see it, has been to reduce the likelihood of our achieving coordination of government in this metropolitan area. The public attitude here has become that of leaving metropolitan questions to be decided by these private agencies. As a community, we apparently have abandoned hope of establishing a metropolitan general government to do our planning or anything else. We depend on private agencies financed and controlled by a small number of big corporations and corporation executives. The rest of the metropolitan community has abdicated.

Look at the record here. In 1929, a county charter to establish a municipal-type government for what was then pretty much the metropolitan area came to a referendum. It received 68 per cent favorable vote but was defeated by a "joker" clause. In 1935 another attempt was made but the charter died in conference committee in the legislature. In 1939, a charter was drafted but no legislator would introduce it. In 1955, the Metropolitan Study Commission, established by the legislature, recommended a "county home rule charter." Nothing at all has been done about that. Back before we had anything resembling metropolitan planning, we came near success. More recently, with something more nearly like metropolitan planning by private agencies, we have got less far each time.

Let me sum it up this way: Metropolitan planning without metropolitan government (1) proliferates special purpose authorities which further fragment governmental powers, and (2) if done by privately financed and controlled agencies as here, weakens broad-base citizen identification with and concern for the metropolitan community and, therefore, (3) lessens the likelihood of establishing coordinated and comprehensive metropolitan government.

The state government, of course, may do metropolitan planning and implement the plans, but I do not like to see the state deciding matters of local concern for a metropolitan community any more than for a city or a borough. If a metropolitan community really exists, that community should have a general government through which to plan and to implement the plans. We kid ourselves or we generate more difficulties if we try to do metropolitan planning without first facing up to the tough political problem of establishing a government with appropriate jurisdiction.

Notes from the Discussion Period

Mr. Gutheim: I certainly agree with you, Mr. Gow, about the evils of proliferation of individual, single-purpose authorities and the lack of popular control, but your counter-arguments may be less valid than you think. Here in Pittsburgh, your proposals were made by outside agencies, not by a metropolitan planning agency. No metropolitan planning has yet been done in this area. You have no basis locally, I contend, to show that real regional or metropolitan planning would not pave the way for metropolitan government.

The Detroit metropolitan area planning organization, though informally organized with the support of small and large local governments, has been effective in developing cooperation, in developing popular approval and support, and has paved the way for state legislation in the direction of metropolitan area needs.

As for the problem of special purpose authorities, I

would agree with you that there are too many of them, that they take decisions away from where they ought to be made, and that they are difficult to control and to coordinate. One good example sticks in my mind: the Port of New York Authority lobbied in the New Jersey legislature against being given responsiblity for inter-urban transit because it felt that its primary responsibility was not to serve the public or the public needs but to protect the bondholders and their investment.

As for the problem of the rural-dominated legislature (is it really rural or is it suburban-dominated?) we are learning how to deal with such legislatures, and I hope we will make more and more progress in the direction. For one thing the urban people are spreading out in the countryside and demanding more and more services there. For another, the suburbs are facing the same problems as the central city, and becoming more sympathetic to the need for cooperation.

Question: Should the state government establish programs for metropolitan planning so as to point the way until an official metropolitan planning agency is established locally?

Mr. Gutheim: Yes.

Mr. Gow: If the boroughs and townships persist in preventing metropolitan planning from coming about, I think that the state should do so. But I should prefer to see it accomplished from the bottom up, from the lowest possible level of approval. If it cannot be done that way, I think that the state should step in and show the way.

Mr. Gutheim: The state should also have a planning agency for broad, over-all planning at the state level to guide and coordinate state programs, as in Tennessee, but there is also a need for problem-solving planning programs at the metropolitan and regional levels in which the state might participate. In Maryland the state legislature is about to consider establishing a state Bureau of Urban Affairs.

Dean Stone: How can planning be brought into focus as an issue?

Mr. Gutheim: Planning per se is not usually an issue (except for budgets and the like). It is the things that planning proposes and the needs of the community that planning tries to meet that become issues. The answer is usually to bring the future into the present by relating immediate problems and programs to the long-range planning solutions. This is the kind of thing that the planner should be adept at as part of his training and experience.

Mr. Knox: We have found that we sometimes avoid issues in government by bringing in outside consultants and authorities to help develop factual studies and proposals and then get action from the state legislature. For example, in recent years the need for better health facilities in the city led to a detailed study of the entire problem in its broad aspects. The program that resulted had bipartisan support and a County Health Department was created. The bipartisan study committee helped to take the issue out of politics.

Mr. Gutheim: Of course there are various techniques for achieving such an end. The development of mutual interests among central city and suburbs can lead to some levels of cooperation—on highways, for example. As an illustration, in the Washington area, the traffic and highway people meet regularly to discuss mutual problems of control mechanisms, laws, and the relating of plans. One finds that novel solutions to regional problems are being developed in many places—Miami, Toronto, Tokyo, and so forth. Some of these experiments deserve careful watching.

Chapter Seven

Planning Organization and Activities Within the Framework of Urban Government

by Henry Fagin
Executive Director, Penn-Jersey Transportation Study

The purpose of organizing and carrying out planning activities within the framework of urban government is to enable the urban community to make intelligent and coherent decisions about its own physical, social, and economic evolution.

Speaking broadly, planning is simply deciding in advance what to do. In this important sense planning is (1) inseparable from deciding; (2) a pre-condition to rational action; and (3) an action-focused activity.

Governmental decisions about the urban community are made typically by a multiplicity of governmental organizations. Planning is an activity of the people who decide matters within them. But the making of decisions actually is diffused throughout urban organizations. Everyone in them makes decisions about what to do, at least in terms of his own activities. Hence, planning is necessarily diffused throughout each organization. Every person in it and each organizational unit does some of the planning.

Nevertheless, we can define also a specialized activity of planning that is distinct from the diffuse planning done constantly by each man at his job. This distinct activity is the basis of a definable planning discipline and profession. Two of its essences are *disciplined research* and *creative invention*. (These are not present in any significant degree in the casual planning of the typical operative.)

But the individual craftsman does exercise both of these functions in regard to his own job when he stops his handiwork for an appreciable interval to take stock and to lay out the longer sequences of his work. When the cooperative efforts of substantial number of persons are involved, however, some degree of planning specialization by particular persons takes place. This does not eliminate all planning by operative personnel, but it does enable the handling of certain aspects of the planning more effectively. What is more significant, a new dimension beyond research and creative invention is brought into the planning: *the coordination of the activities of many individuals.*

In a large and complex organization one is apt to find a hierarchy of centers in which specialized planning (among other administrative functions) takes place. Whether this planning is done as a part-time activity of someone who also has other functions or as a full-time activity of one or more persons identifiable as planners in the professional sense depends on the scale and character of the operations served by a particular administrative center.

FIVE FUNCTIONS OF PLANNING:

1. Research and Information

The gathering, analyzing, and reporting of facts is a basic planning function. Within the framework of urban government these facts include conditions, activities, trends, opinions, experiences, and other aspects of urban life. The facts describe the physical, social, economic, and political aspects of the urban environment. They encompass the substance of governmental programs but they extend also to all the factors in the nongovernmental sector that have a substantial bearing on governmental activities.

2. General Goal Formation

Another fundamental planning function is the formation of general goals. The development of general goals involves a process of interaction among three groups: (1) the public and its voluntary organizations, (2) government as expressed by the elected representatives and their appointive administrative officials, and (3) the professional and technical aides and consultants who staff urban planning offices. General goals for governmental action are the result of decisions made throughout this system of interactions.

Some decisions about goals inevitably are made within the specialized planning offices themselves. (This happens, for example, when someone in a planning office eliminates a particular alternative from further consideration by omitting it from a report.) Yet, the major influences that shape general governmental goals act mainly outside the confines of planning agencies. To be precise we should say that a planning office participates in general goal formation along with the other parties. Its contribution, however, is important and unique.

3. Specific Plan Making

In addition to participating in the formation of general goals, a planning office plays a part also in the preparation of more specific goals—goals sufficiently different in certain respects to warrant a verbal distinction. We call these specific goals *plans*. The *making of plans* is in fact the *pivotal* function of a planning office whether it be at the bureau, departmental, or central administrative level.

The word *plan* has several different meanings. As used here it serves as a general term for *a coordinated system of some kind intended as a guide to action*. For example, a plan expressing desired space relations is called a master plan, design plan, general plan, comprehensive plan, or physical development plan. A plan expressing economic factors such as the desirable relationships between projections of resources and of service requirements is called a financial plan or budget. A plan proposing a coordinated system of activities is called a plan of action or more commonly a program. Each of these is a coordinated system intended as a guide to action.

A plan which is comprehensive of all *three* kinds of systems and which, moreover, brings physical, social, and economic considerations into a common focus is a special new type of plan. Currently this new instrument is being evolved in several municipalities, agencies, and industrial corporations. It is called a *policies plan,* and in the near future its preparation and maintenance will become, I believe, the fundamental expression of the plan-making function of a planning office. I believe that the theories and skills necessary to the making of policies plans should constitute the central core of planning education.

4. Coordination

Coordination is a fourth planning function. A planning office effects coordination in at least three important ways. First, it induces coordination by the way it organizes and reports its factual research. The figures published, the trends established, and the standards expressed all tend to become the common assumptions underlying what many other bodies do. Second, the work of a planning office facilitates coordination by providing a center of liaison. Work on the policies plan requires a planning office to maintain many points of contact with other groups and organizations. It is thus able to enlist the voluntary cooperation of many individuals and groups in the coordination of matters on which a natural consensus is easily reached. And third, the primary work of a planning office on the policies plan of the governmental unit it serves has a strong coordinative impact on the goals, plans, and programs which comprise the policies plan.

The coordinative function of planning is addressed to a number of distinct sets of interrelations. These include:

(1) The relations among the persons or groups whose cooperative activities are directly served by the particular planning office (the planning office of a large recreation department, for example).

(2) The relations between the given planning office and other coordinate planning offices (as for example among the planning offices of departments within a municipal government or among the planning offices of a number of municipalities in a metropolitan region).

(3) The relations between the given planning office and those of either lower or higher levels of government.

(4) The relations between the given governmental planning office and those of quasi-governmental agencies, private enterprises, or voluntary organizations.

Of course it is important to recognize also a limit to a planning office's coordination influence. All sorts of negotiations, compromises, and adjustments in plans are necessary in the course of bringing a satisfactory degree of coherence to the interrelated activities of these various interacting parties. While some of the modifications fall well within the range of discretion normally delegated to planning officers, other accommodations require the exercise of a quality of policy power beyond what is appropriate to staff appointees. This is one of the major reasons why a planning office benefits greatly from serving within the structure of government as a direct arm of the executive officer who *is* responsible for the pertinent ultimate executive policy decisions. This principle applies equally at the departmental and central levels. Such an organizational location just below a top executive officer tends to promote an easy flow of planning decisions.

In addition to the foregoing coordinative functions, a planning office performs another crucial aspect of coordination: namely, coordination of events in *time*. Planning always has to do with actions not yet taken. It is important that future events be synchronized, that the provision of services and facilities in the future be geared to future requirements and resources.

5. Assistance and Advice

A further valuable planning function consists of furnishing assistance and advice—this based on the special knowledge, experience, and background of the planning personnel. This assistance and advice may be extended "downward" to line operatives and to subordinate or more local agencies. Conversely, they may be extended "upward" to more central or embracive units of government. And they may be offered also to nongovernmental enterprises and private persons.

THE SCOPE OF GOVERNMENTAL PLANNING

In scope I believe governmental planning is as broad as the concerns of government. It includes governmental activities being planned and their underlying considerations. This scope encompasses the physical, social, and economic evolution of the environment. The governmental and private sectors of urban development are closely entwined and interdependent. Hence, in theory at least, governmental planning must take into account not only the things government does directly but also the much larger range of things affecting and affected by governmental activity. In practice, of course, a high degree of selectivity is necessary. This is so both because many communities desire a deliberate scaling-down toward a minimum of governmental involvement and because of the sheer unwieldiness of the whole mass of public and private action. The reasoned determination of where to cut off in the endless chain of public and private interaction is one of the important planning problems.

It should be noted at this point perhaps that some members of the American Institute of Planners—possibly today even a majority—would propose to limit the scope of what they would call governmental planning to things which can be expressed in terms of the arrangement of land uses. To me this seems an unnecessary and probably harmful effort to appropriate the common word, planning, for the exclusive use of a narrow segment of the planners in government.

THE PLACEMENT OF PLANNING WITHIN THE GOVERNMENTAL FRAMEWORK

Planning is done by many kinds of persons and not merely by professional planners or planning staffs. Some —mayors, managers, and department heads, for ex-ample—have main administrative responsibilties which are broader than planning. These officials also direct, control, organize, and administer. Planning is an in-cidental activity also for persons at the operating levels and their supervisors. It is the *central* activity, however, for certain persons in government—planning officers and their staffs (by whatever names they may be known, such as finance officers, budget directors, planning engineers, construction coordinators, AIP planners, or just plan-ners). The planning profession and its subdivisions are concerned with work these people do. How are they best worked into the structure of urban government?

Ultimate decisions about what urban governments shall and shall not do rest heavily on legislative action. Legislatures are, among other things, planning bodies. Nevertheless, the major content of governmental pro-grams can be developed only through a substantial involvement of the executive arm and the whole array of administrative agencies reporting upward to the ex-ecutive. In a formal sense, then, the basic planning func-tion, *the making of plans,* must be a direct responsibility of the chief executive.

There may exist some governments so simple in structure and small in size as not to have any one official recognizable as the top executive of the municipal ad-ministration. In virtually all modern urban govern-ments, however, some top executive will be found. This person may be a directly elected mayor, an elective official selected from among the members of the legislative body, an appointive official serving as manager or chief administrative officer, or someone else.

Whatever his method of designation, however, his integral ties to the operations of the government and his responsibility for coordinating governmental activities make it essential that the top executive play a preeminent role in the exercise of the planning function. Depending on the size and complexity of the government, he may do the planning himself (among his other activities) or he may carry it out through one or more subordinates. Again, depending on the size and complexity of *their* responsibilities, these subordinate officials may or may not further subdivide and delegate their planning responsibilities.

I find it helpful to visualize a whole universe of centers of planning when thinking about planning organization. In considering the following discussion of this universe of planning centers in urban government, one should constantly bear in mind the distinction just made between the exercise of the planning function by all sorts of persons on the one hand and the matter of organizational specialization for planning by planners in the professional sense on the other hand. What may appear in my description as an unusually elaborate array of planning centers actually often is concealed within quite simple governmental structures.

Let us begin by looking at typical operating departments in local government. Each plans certain things within its delegated jurisdiction and each formulates plans for consideration by a more centrally situated planning office. Insofar as physical, social, economic, and political factors enter the planning, there is need to draw on persons competent in these special aspects of planning respectively to participate in the departmental planning. Hence, at least at various recurrent intervals in time, a diversified planning group will be at work at the departmental level. The full array of such departmental planning groups may be likened to a ring of satellites forming a circle, with the central administrative unit of the municipality at the center. In our analogy this would be similar to Jupiter and its moons.

At the municipal administrative center, under the aegis of the chief executive, the central planning office is at work forming or modifying plans—some for further action by the departments or by the central administrative unit itself, some for consideration by other governmental jurisdictions, such as the municipal legislative body, the county, and the state. Within the governmental structure of urban counties, a similar set of satellite and central points of planning concentration may be discerned.

The municipalities and counties in turn may be regarded as a planet-like ring of planning centers oriented to a metropolitan government—the metropolitan solar system's sun. And the latter, if it is to function effectively as a governmental entity, requires, in addition to municipal planets, its own satellite circle of metropolitan-level operating departments or agencies with individual planning centers of their own. It also needs to have a principal central metropolitan planning office. The state and federal levels of planning extend the analogy to other stars and galaxies.

At each of the centers of planning identified above there is a need to organize the triple processes of disciplined research, creative invention, and activity coordination so as to carry out the various planning functions. As has already been stressed, the degree to which the necessary activities are articulated by the assignment of specialized personnel depends on the scale of operations. It will be easiest to analyze the components of a planning office, however, if we consider a large one in which the various activities are embodied in distinct persons and organizational divisions. But the conception presented applies equally to all planning offices—even those at the extreme which consist only of the part-time attention of a one-man operation.

Among the functions of the chief executive of a unit of urban government several responsibilities form a planning cluster. These include the generation and development of such things as governmental activity programs, regulatory enactments, construction programs, and financial programs. The planning cluster may be distinguished from other executive functions like supervision, direction, and control.

It is my own view that in a large and complex organization the planning cluster should be given organizational recognition. A *planning office,* so named, should be established. It should be headed by an appointive planning officer, a deputy of the chief executive reporting directly to him.

Despite the desirability of flexibility in grouping personnel for particular tasks, the basic organization of a planning office probably should recognize some permanent underlying structure. In most municipalities this is done now by an extreme fragmentation of planning into separate offices. So sharp are these separations into organizational units, wholly independent of each other, that joint work is very hard to achieve. Budgeting specialists, physical planning specialists, and program development specialists generally are attached to distinct budget, physical planning, and programming offices respectively. A spirit of rivalry and competition is more common than a practice of easy collaboration.

In my view what is needed is to bring these planning specialties together within a single unified planning office. *Within* the office, however, perhaps the basic organizational subdivisions should be primarily along the lines of professional specialization. Thus, for example, the budgeting, fiscal, economic, and financial analysis specialists should be responsible to the head planning officer through a top financial planning chief. Similarly, the specialists in land development controls, land planning, and urban design perhaps should be responsible to the head planning officer through a top physical planning chief. And certain specialties necessary for developing the general content of municipal programs should be grouped under a program planning chief who reports to the head planning officer.

During the course of a typical year, however, it probably would be desirable to group and re-group the personnel of the planning office in various combinations depending on the requirements of particular work projects. It is important that all of the work done bear the impress of competent thinking with regard to whatever considerations are present. Physical, social, economic, and political aspects alike must be thoroughly understood and expressed.

This might be accomplished best with respect to certain types of projects by the assembly of special project teams staffed by a mixture of planning specialists. In the case of other projects, however, which fall mainly under some particular competence, occasional consultation and review by other specialists may be sufficient. Thus, for example, the budget might be the primary responsibility of a financial planning division of the planning office, with occasional contributions from the other specialists, while the long-range physical plan or the municipal design plan might be the primary responsibility of a physical planning division. (It was suggested above that particular officials may function part of the time as members of one organizational unit and at other times within other units. Thus, the view that the chief budget officer should be an important member of the planning office does not preclude his alignment for certain purposes with other financial officers such as the controller.)

BASIC INSTRUMENTS OF URBAN PLANNING

The professional work of urban planning is accomplished through two main kinds of instruments: the first, *plans* expressed in the form of documents; the second, *committee work* through which a substantial amount of coordination is achieved.

To date, almost invariably, the physical, economic, and social policies of urban governments have been developed largely in fragments and in isolation from each other. It is true that a degree of discipline is being brought into financial planning through the instrumentality of budgets (though seldom are these comprehensive of all resources and financial requirements). Similarly, a degree of discipline is being introduced into physical planning through the development of physical master plans. As to the orderly balancing of governmental activity programs, no direct instruments have yet been put to general use. Such programs are integrated, if at all, indirectly through the budget or through plans for physical improvements designed to accommodate activity programs.

A new instrument capable of bringing all these aspects of governmental planning into a single disciplining framework appears to be needed. And the concept of a *policies plan* currently is being developed to meet this need.

A policies plan would be a unified document adopted in order to express the intended general goals, specific

117

plans, and programs for urban growth and change. Each urban governmental entity, whether a local municipality, county, or metropolitan district, would benefit from having a policies plan of its own. Such an instrument would enable it to bring its policy ideas into a reasonable state of coherence as well as to register and communicate adjustments in policy agreed upon after conference and negotiation. The policies plan would express in one place the social, economic, physical, and political policies intended to guide the evolution of the particular area of governmental jurisdiction. It would contain physical plans coordinating spatial relationships; schedules coordinating time relationships; budgets coordinating financial relationships; and narrative texts and tables describing and coordinating proposed activity programs. Maps, schedules, and texts also would set forth the physical, economic, and social facts, assumptions, and goals underlying the governmental policies.

The preparation of the policies plan would be a major responsibility of the central planning office of an urban government. This work would be done, however, in collaboration with the other planning centers of the government as well as with those of other local, metropolitan, state, federal governments and agencies.

The important multi-way interaction among planners in the many planning centers of an urban area would not be achieved without conscious effort. It probably would be aided materially by the organization of continuing committees of the respective top planning officers of these centers. Such committees would provide regular and convenient opportunities for consulting on problems of interrelationships and coordination.

A regular exchange of policy plans within the framework of such committees would introduce an entirely

118

new dimension into metropolitan cooperation. It would enable the assembly and juxtaposition of the individual goals of the many public (and even private) organizations, departments, agencies, and other bodies which interact to effect metropolitan change. This very act of juxtaposition itself inevitably would identify unintended inconsistencies, inadequacies, and interferences among the various plans. Doubtless it would result in a significant degree of voluntary coordination through a process of mutual adjustment on the part of the parties whose goals would thus be found to be in unnecessary conflict.

THE GOVERNMENT OF METROPOLITAN REGIONS

This has been a discussion of "planning organization and activities within the framework of urban government." It might be appropriate to close with a thought about a major shortcoming of urban government in the United States. The passage just above suggests that a significant degree of coherence might be achieved in our metropolitan regions through the voluntary efforts of the appointive officials and professionals who staff urban planning offices. It should be noted, however, that two elements are missing which would be essential to achieving an appreciable degree of *metropolitan* coordination: a metropolitan policies plan and a metropolitan planning office.

If one reflects back on the process by which a policies plan would have to be created and adopted, it becomes clear that this can occur only through the workings of a responsible unit of government wherein political questions may be resolved and authentic decisions made. This matter was the subject of study during the past year within the American Institute of Planners by a

National Policy Committee on Metropolitan Planning. In the words of the committee report:

In most metropolitan regions there are some questions which should be decided by the metropolitan constituency itself rather than by the state or federal government or by the local governments separately. . . .

In general the highest levels of coordinated metropolitan planning will be able to occur only after some form of metropolitan government has been established; for only in the context of unified governmental structure can there be achieved the fullest collaboration among public and private agencies and a regular and responsible resolution of many conflicting interests leading to effective action.

Comments by Joseph M. Heikoff

Associate Professor of Regional Planning, University of Illinois

I would like to address myself to some questions of planning organization suggested by Mr. Fagin's comments.

Mr. Fagin has urged that the planning office should be an integral part of the executive branch of local government directly responsible to the chief executive. This is the situation that already exists in some cities, but planning operations started out quite differently. Modern community planning is only a little over fifty years old, and at the beginning of the century it wasn't even recognized as a function of government. Civic clubs and dedicated individuals assumed leadership in this field and financed the making of plans for communities with their own funds. The Burnham plan for Chicago is perhaps the best known example. Chicago also set the stage for promotion by civic leaders of the "city beautiful" with its famous World's Fair of that period. In fairness to the Burnham plan, however, I

121

should note that it was concerned about economic and social problems as well as community appearance.

Interest in this aspect of city planning, which favored the development of civic centers, parks, and public monuments, was broadened by the appearance of civic committees generally supported by local business interests. Some of these committees engaged technical staffs and even received some assistance from public funds, but they had no official relationship to government itself. Incidentally, we should be grateful to this movement for the great park systems, museums, and public recreation facilities that some of our cities boast of today.

Within a couple of decades, technical and civic leaderships in this field developed to the point where city planning was made an official activity, although not integrated completely into the governmental structure. The scandals that brought to light widespread corruption in local government brought about agitation for reform. Planning was considered too sensitive a function to be entrusted to politicians so planning responsibility, and sometimes power, were vested in an independent commission. The members were given overlapping terms that were longer than the terms of the mayors who appointed them. The idea was to take planning out of politics and give it continuity.

Planning responsibilities in many states are still exercised by this kind of organization, as established by state enabling legislation, city charters, and local laws. Before the planning commission can be abolished and its powers and responsibilities distributed between the legislature and the chief executive, changes in state and local legislation will be required in many areas.

Mr. Fagin has noted how loosely we use the word planning. Many of the people who claim that they are professional planners nevertheless insist on limiting themselves only to consideration of the physical environment. I agree with Mr. Fagin that this is a misappropriation of the word planning. Community planning, it seems to me, by definition includes all of the activities that government has to make decisions about. Decisions about land use, development, and control, as well as the design and location of community facilities, are only part of the community plan, which must relate these environmental aspects to the government's program of public services and to its operating and capital budgets.

On the basis of this definition of terms, I suggest that there should be two kinds of planning offices in local government. One would be a *line department,* and it would carry out specific operating responsibilities such as administration of zoning appeals, administration of subdivision regulations, and, perhaps, even the operation of urban renewal and public housing programs.

The other kind of planning office would be a *staff agency* to do research and to coordinate the government's development, operating, and financial programs. The responsibilities of this office would extend to the making of the land-use plan, community facilities plan, and financial plan—as instruments of coordination, as well as recommendations for regulatory legislation and other controls.

My experience has been that planning agency heads who are responsible for both of these kinds of activities find that they are pressured into devoting most of their time and energy to the operating side. Cities existed for a long time before zoning was thought of and put into operation. A zoning ordinance has to impose reasonable controls over old areas and at the same time raise standards for new ones. Since the ordinance cannot go into detail about how it would be applied to every piece of property, there arise many problems of adjudication. These problems require that the planning agency head try to resist pressure from politicians, placate property owners, and keep the Board of Appeals in line so they will not grant variances that in effect amend the ordinance. Subdividers also want to see the boss and dress him down for making them reduce the number of lots or improve street design and make improvements in their area. Urban renewal and other kinds of project planning bring their own headaches. All these operating pressures leave the planning director little time and energy to see to his agency's research and coordinating activities.

Some planning agencies have tried to act as both line and staff units at the same time, but I do not believe they have generally been successful. It seems to me that an operating "Department of Community Development" and a staff "Bureau of Plan Coordination"—you can change the names to suit your own preferences—are both needed in a city of any size. Planners with special talents and training would be attracted more to one or the other of these kinds of agencies. Mr. Fagin has pointed out that planning is necessarily diffused throughout each organization, and it is perhaps unfair of one group to call themselves the planners, especially when they only do part of the organization's planning. I suspect that other government executives resent the use of this label and do not like the implication that they are to be planned by the planners. If we can talk about community development and plan coordination—which would include recognition of everybody's contribution to governmental planning—then perhaps we can remove some of the barriers to communication between the "planners" and other government officials.

Whatever the scope and organization of the planning agency, its success will most likely depend upon the personal relationships that develop between the planning agency head and the chief executive, operating department heads and other responsible officials, and the public.

In most communities there are at present two separate, and sometimes conflicting, planning operations. One goes on in the chief executive's office, and he runs it with an executive committee or a formal or informal staff group (such as a "kitchen cabinet" of unofficial advisers). This is planning in the broad sense which I think Mr. Fagin gives the term, for this is where goals are really formulated, alternatives explored, and decisions on action actually made.

Some professional city planners do not recognize this as planning at all, and they label this kind of thing "politics." Many of them seem afraid of it and try to keep away from the chief executive's office for this reason. They want to have a nice little operation of their own with the sign "Planning Office" on the door, but which is concerned with only a narrow segment of the governmental planning process. Very often this kind of operation is not of much real help to the chief executive and he tends to ignore it. On the other hand, there are some professionals who are more versatile in their approach and who would like to offer more effective participation in the councils of government; but they are hampered by administrative separation from the chief executive, intervening commissions, and the frequent conception by the chief executive of the planning office as a necessary nuisance.

I don't suppose that the separation of these two kinds

of planning operation will be easily overcome but it seems to me desirable that it should.

Notes from the Discussion Period:

Q. Granted the desirability of what you have out-lined, Mr. Fagin, how do we move from the present situation to the one you propose? I am particularly mindful of the difficulty of achieving close relations with other department heads where you seem to be taking over functions that they formerly regarded as theirs, and also the problem of the timing of the policy plan function of the planning department as it may relate to other functions.

Mr. Fagin: It is true that both budget specialists and planning specialists have lacked a proper understanding of their own roles in relation to other officials. But collaboration has been worked out in connection with capital improvement programs in many places; and I can see no reason why, if the mayor and council want this kind of joint work, it cannot be accomplished satisfactorily.

At the National Planning Conference held in Pittsburgh in 1952, Walter Blucher and City Manager Bean debated the importance of the Planning Commission. Six important functions it fulfills were listed:

Buffer between staff director and both the public and the officials

Buffer between elected officials and the public

Deliberative body (sounding board)

Supervising body for planning staff

Coordinating body

Long-range thinking group

Not one of these functions in my opinion should be separated from the executive and legislative bodies of the community itself. The buffers are an undesirable insulation; and responsibility for the other functions should be placed squarely on the elected officials and their subordinates.

Moreover, I don't think changes of statutes would be necessary in many places; just get a mayor who wants to provide the right kind of leadership and the needed process can generally be initiated by administrative determination.

I think for example of a village in New York. The governmental officials were leery of planners and consultants taking away their power of decision-making. We at the Regional Plan Association were called in for advice, and we suggested the idea of a policies plan and the use of such a plan to control both physical development and administration. This concept was adopted, and subsequent to this both planning and administrative consultants were retained, but with less fear of what they might do to the community over and beyond its own basic legislative control. This experience indicated that all that was needed to resolve the long-standing impasse over planning was the development of an approximate approach.

Q. Do you agree that planning should be divested of the planning commission and made a staff agency in the executive department?

Mr. Fagin: To my mind the existence of the planning commission can prevent full recognition of planning and limit understanding of its proper position in local government. Setting up the department and the program in the terms I suggested will tend to assure such recognition of its role by the chief administrator.

The necessary coordination of planning on all its levels cannot take place unless there is a recognition of the central planning function. For instance, budgeting officers are moving away from the traditional line budgets. Performance budgeting represents the first step and program budgeting the second. But the program contained in the budget is the same thing as that for which physical plans as well as other plans are made.

I also think there are roles to be played by the independent private agencies, such as the Citizens' Planning and Housing Associations in New York and Philadelphia. A responsible, independent, agency can make an important contribution through advice and criticism. In my view, this function of reflecting citizen opinion is better done by a citizens group on its own initiative than by an appointed and hand-picked official lay commission or board.

Q. Do you think the planners actually want to do these things you propose, or do they want to maintain the independence of physical planning as a function remote from government?

Mr. Fagin: There is a difference among planners themselves. You'll find the newer and younger planners (of all ages) better able to take such responsibilities and perform well. But there is also the matter of the ability of the administrator or chief executive in knowing how best to utilize the services of his planner and give him appropriate responsibilities.

Q. Does this mean that the planner is any of the specialists you mentioned or that the planner is the generalist created by rubbing all kinds of disciplines together in a research situation? In other words how would your proposal affect the education and training of planners?

Mr. Fagin: The main thing is that the planner must gain sufficient knowledge of various fields and skills and the ability to utilize them as a generalist. But in addition to the planner in the total situation, you would have to draw on specialists in each of the social, economic, physical, and administrative disciplines that contribute to the planning function. These persons are to be found distributed throughout governmental structures. The planner has to make full use of their expertness—not try to duplicate it.

Chapter Eight

General Planning and Planning for Services and Facilities

by James A. Norton

Professor of Area Development, Case Institute of Technology

Planning has been described as deciding in advance what to do. This is a useful definition in focusing attention on decision-making and looking ahead. It is also general enough to let us bring many different kinds of planning into our consideration. This is necessary to understand our topic for discussion.

Actually, an employee of local government *plans* when he makes out his calendar of activities for a day. Let us take a local public health educator as a case in point. When he arrives in the morning several requests are on his desk. The director of a citizen cancer society has asked that he call to help them plan a drive for early detection; the YMCA is holding a luncheon to discuss recreation for elderly persons; posters have been sketched out for local schools and need his attention; and in the evening two different groups have asked him to make speeches. It would be easy to fill his day just responding to outside requests. Some of these outside demands he must turn down.

To really plan his day he will think through the program of the department. Geriatrics are a major problem and to receive special attention during the year; public participation in sanitary programs is to be emphasized, and so forth. Planning was being done when the department, probably under strong leadership of the director, decided what its program would be for the year. These year-long goals are, hopefully, in line with much longer-range aims, in part dictated by the professional training of the departmental personnel, in part by the personal goals of the individuals involved, in part by the community needs as perceived by the mayor and civic and political leaders.

Many different agents—locally and elsewhere—contribute to this planning. A special program may have been laid out by Congress and funds made available. The state government may have inauguarted an economy drive. Up and down the federal system decisions have been made for future action and, to a degree, the local health educator must integrate those decisions into his own planning process. The more he understands the factors pertinent to his work, the better his planning can be.

He does not need to know all the decisions that have been made, however. Some factors merely set parameters for his work; these same factors may demand decisions for persons on other government levels.

Let us assume he has been operating in a large city from the downtown city hall. Travel takes much of his time and adds to the expense of his work. He has requested more office space and complained about the often fruitless search for neighborhood meeting rooms. The nurse has worried about better housing for their well-child clinic. A case worker in the welfare agency may have been making investigations in a neighborhood far removed from the office. Building inspectors and service department personnel travel miles and miles between office and work.

In the course of his work, the director of the health department decided that a neighborhood health center was needed in neighborhood A. He approached the mayor about it and they agreed on the popularity of the project. The nurses and the health educator knew of some vacant land "just where it ought to be," so that site became a departmental goal.

Now health officers are not unlike many other persons and this department failed completely to take into account where the new freeway was going or what urban renewal was about to do to this neighborhood. They hadn't even heard that since the welfare, recreation, and the housing departments were all seeking quarters in that region that the administrative officer had broached the subject of decentralized "regional service centers" for different departments that did a great deal of field work. And not one of them could know the storm that would break when it was suggested that building inspectors not be headquartered directly under the eye of their chief. (They were aware of the fact that the finance director thought the city did not have a single extra cent that year.)

This parable has gone on too long, but there should be ample evidence that some over-all planning would be quite proper here. This does not imply that all these problems would be solved if there were a planning department. As a matter of fact, it would not be too unusual to find that the planners had made some very pretty pictures without even asking about whether their proposals really helped to set a framework to assist the various departments in meeting the needs of the community. But with this as a background, let me outline a few of the relationships which I think should prevail. There are six points I want especially to make about the various facets of planning.

First, daily work programs should be designed to accomplish over-all aims of the departments and the government. In an outline on "The Tasks of Management" which has been prepared by Dean Donald Stone there is a very comprehensive list of activities that "are carried on simultaneously and . . . represent a continuous and changing process." Definition of objectives and planning programs to carry out the objectives are the first two major headings. At no time are the objectives or the programs static, but they are related constantly and integrated vertically and horizontally with other programs in local, state, and national governments. Daily work programs are influenced by, but also influence, over-all objectives and their implementation. This observation is commonplace, but its implications are important.

Second, within the master plan, the planning department must include plans for facilities for all departments. How can a master plan be constructed unless it includes such things as housing for major activities and centers that facilitate administrative decentralization when that is a policy? Similarly, how can a department plan for its work in a neighborhood without knowing that there will be neighborhoods, or that population shifts of such and such a type are in the offing? The inclusion of items such as these is important to the operating departments; it is equally useful to planners.

No one should assume that the planner knows just what the facilities should be without consultation with the departments. Nor should one assume that the departments really know what they need over the next planning period. Planning must be cooperative every step of the way, and the best planners will try to involve the operating departments just as they would involve citizen groups. Planners can help the agencies come to understand their own needs. When operating departments present blue-sky thinking or vague requests, pertinent questions should be asked: "Is this realistic from a fiscal point of view? Have you forgotten to ask for parking space around your new health center? What are the implications for your program of our latest population projections? Etc."

Our *third* admonition is closely related to this one: A realistic capital program and annual capital budgets must be tools for the whole government to use. Philadelphia has set a high standard in the field of capital programming and budgeting. An annual capital budget is prepared with the capital program for the next five years. The many different departments must cooperate with the planners in developing the programs and budgets and the council must take formal action before they come into operation.

Without some tools such as these, planning is weak in its implementation, and rational decisions in council control of money is virtually impossible. Take the matter of determining priorities in capital expenditures. Obviously there should be a legitimate need before money is expended. There also should be political support for the project. But needs are unlimited and political support can be found for almost anything. Only in the capital budget process are the many relevant questions asked. For example: If this expenditure is postponed, will it become more expensive later? Or will it be unnecessary? Or will it be impossible to accomplish the aim it is designed for? Would the new facilities save operating funds enough to amortize their cost? Or will they seriously overburden an already strained budget? Is there any money available? How does it fit into other programs? Are federal funds available that will soon disappear? Or will more funds become available next year?

The scores of questions that are part of capital programming and budgeting are probably asked best by a planning agency that has an overview of the complete governmental program. Part of the duty of the planning agency is to help the operating departments move ahead when the time is best and to encourage patience when action is impossible.

The capital budget must be coordinated with the operating budget every step of the way. This is the *fourth* point that should be made. Capital planning that leaves out this important dimension could hardly be called planning.

Fifth, if planning is to fulfill its greatest role, it must be regarded as a team function, and the planner as a team member. Planning demands economic and demographic sophistication; it demands an understanding of how land uses are related, how commerce and industry and residence are tied together by transportation, and the impact of each of these on the other. It demands a comprehension of finance—of taxing and spending and borrowing; and it demands an understanding of administration and politics—of communications and decision-making. *Not one* of these elements can be omitted any more than can civic design and a feeling for spatial relationships and the good life.

In a large planning agency these skills—and the others that are needed—may be emphasized in different sections, or at least in different persons. Where this is the case, it is essential that the planning director be a skilled administrator to see that the team function is comprehensive. The planning must be an *organization* product.

In a small planning agency, one person may be required to embody all these skills. Needless to say he can never know all he needs to know. But his education must have made him aware of the many facets of his work; he should not be ignorant of a map or a budget and he should recognize that one represents as high an art as the other.

In large and small agencies it is imperative that the planner recognize his relationship to other departments. He must seek to understand their needs if he is to coordinate them. He must have good communications horizontally across the government hierarchy as well as up and down into the centers of decision.

It is always necessary, it seems, to point out that while the role which has been described is an active one, it should never be allowed to destroy its *raison d'être*—which is planning. The planning director must be aware of the seductive nature of day-by-day problems and maintain his planning perspective, redefining it to the operating departments and to the executive and legislature as needed.

A *sixth* and last comment seems to be in order as we think about metropolitan planning. Almost by definition there is a multiplicity of governmental units in a metropolitan area. Each of these governments does its own programming, often oblivious of all the others until there is an actual clash. Planners must recognize (in their actions as well as theory) that the other governments are "givens" in their planning just as is the topography of the area, though certainly less predictable in future behavior!

This is to suggest that the planners should communicate with other governments as to what their plans are. Knowing what bond issues are to be presented by overlying school or park districts may be important in establishing the capital budget. Knowing where land is to be acquired may make cooperative programs possible. While there are limitations to the possibilities in this field, many serious metropolitan problems could have been anticipated and made less serious if the planners had included other governments in the area as data pertinent to their problems.

The planner, to do his best job, must have a breadth of knowledge in the field of government that is difficult to overstate. What he does not know from his own training, he must appreciate and respect in others. The ramifications of his task reach into the whole of government activity. This is why his job is so challenging and so satisfying.

GENERAL PLANNING AND PLANNING FOR
SERVICES AND FACILITIES

Summary of Panel Discussion by

Donald C. Stone
Dean, Graduate School of Public and International Affairs
University of Pittsburgh

James A. Norton
Professor of Area Development, Case Institute of Technology

John J. Matthews
Executive Director, Allegheny County Planning Department
Pennsylvania

In the discussion of the several questions posed during the course of the seminar session, certain general
areas of agreement became apparent. These conclusions,
for the most part, represent a composite of the views
expressed by each of the panel participants.

1. The Central Planning Agency's Relationships with Operation Departments

The extent to which the central planning agency concerns itself with operating departments and programs
depends upon the community's "Master Plan"—how it is
defined, how much detail it contains as to location of
facilities, programs for effectuation, priorities, and the
like. Perhaps, even more importantly, it also will depend upon the position occupied by the planning
agency in the governmental hierarchy. If the planning
function is conceived as a staff arm of the executive, the

answer will likely be different from that expressed in the case of the semi-autonomous or independent commission.

The extent to which the planning agency *can* occupy itself with these matters is the more important issue, for, if planning is to achieve its maximum effectiveness as a tool of administration, e.g., a staff facility, there must be a basis for continuing cooperation between the central planning agency and the operating departments.

One panel member stated that where an operating department has not, or cannot, clearly define its program and objectives, it may become necessary for the planning agency to make decisions for the department, but that this practice of decision-making by default can lead only to involvement in management at the expense of planning. He felt that the functions of the planning agency should be confined to physical facilities only.

In support of the thesis expressed by Mr. Fagin in his session that the central planning agency should concern itself with the budget process and similar management functions, the others were of the opinion that more and more, the planning agency is moving, and will continue to move, into the area of management. Capital improvements programming, which is gaining increasing recognition as a function of the central planning agency, was cited as an example of the trend toward greater emphasis in management activities. This movement, it was held, eventually will have its impact upon the type of person selected to direct the planning operation and upon the kinds of persons employed to fill some of the principal positions.

2. *Capital Improvements Programs*

Eventually, every community must recognize the necessity for programming its capital improvements over a longer period than provided for in its annual operating budget. Ideally, the program should involve at least these eight basic considerations:

(1) Knowledge of the direction in which the community is moving in order to anticipate the physical facilities that will be needed. Most appropriately, the master plan should include all the items appearing in the capital improvements program. Whether a comprehensive plan exists or not, each operating department should define its long-range objectives and identify the specific facilities it will need to achieve its purposes.

(2) Knowledge of the total financial resources of the community so that needs may be related to ability to pay. In addition to considering the sources of revenue presently utilized, it is necessary to determine the additional sources of funds that may be available. Too often a program is unnecessarily weakened or limited because it is developed solely within the framework of the existing revenue structure. Expenditures, revenue sources, and purposes are political decisions that must finally be made by the publicly responsible, elected official. However, the persons developing the improvements program must provide all the facts necessary for intelligent decision-making by the executive and the city legislative body.

(3) A five- or six-year improvement plan is necessary to coordinate properly the program for meeting public needs. The process of compiling the program requires that priorities be established for the various improvements. Whatever their social and economic values, the proposals must also possess political virtues, perhaps even going so far as to provide "something for everybody."

(4) The effect of the capital improvements program

on the operating budget must be considered. Each new facility must at least be maintained, and many will necessitate additional expenditures for expanded services. Because capital improvements programs will inevitably require continuing commitments for operation, the operating and capital budgets should be integrated into a single fiscal program; otherwise financial stability and the possibilities for substantial savings may be considerably reduced.

(5) At least the major projects must be documented in detail. Preliminary plans including cost estimates are essential if the projects are to be programmed precisely and in accordance with available funds.

(6) The scheduling of the program often must take into consideration the need for project approval by many outside agencies and the amount of time that will elapse before such approvals can be secured. Some capital items may run the gamut of intergovernmental arrangements and negotiations with private interests that may require years to complete. Careful timing is essential if each part of the program is to be constructed in harmony with all the related portions. It is equally important the construction take place in accordance with the schedule established in the improvements plan. Too often, operating departments over-estimate the amount of work they are capable of performing. It must be recognized that every construction program is a complicated process that may require additional personnel to carry it out.

(7) There is need for coordinating the capital improvements programs of the various governmental

units providing services in the urban area. One successful technique has been the use of civic organizations representing the local power structure to serve on the capital program committees of the various political jurisdictions. Their involvement not only enhances the opportunities for achieving effective coordination of activities, but aids immeasurably in securing the approval of the electorate for bond issues as well.

(8) The programming of capital improvements must be recognized as a continuing function, one that is never completed. Each year, the program should be evaluated, appraised, and, when necessary, revised or revamped. At the completion of the current year's operations, an additional year must be added so that the schedule always represents a work program for the four-or-five-year period that lies ahead.

3. Work Programming

Work programming as it applies to municipal facilities and services is primarily the concern of the budget director, but it also is of importance to the planning official responsible for the development of capital programs. Objectives must be clearly and precisely defined. The definition of objectives is, perhaps, the least developed and the most involved of any task of management, and, their lack, the principal cause of administrative failure. Together with the definition of objectives, the development of measures of units of work and units of cost should be the basis for both capital and operating budgets.

Work and cost unit data reflected in performance budgets are invaluable for internal management in the preparation and implementation of plans, in guiding the operating departments in the exercise of their current and long-range activities, and in achieving a harmonious pattern of operation and activity. They facilitate legislative consideration of the budget with attention focused on policy and program issues rather than on details of expenditure.

4. *Local Services in a Metropolitan Area*

To protect and promote the interests of the citizens of an urban complex, it is necessary to insist that minimum levels of certain services be provided, perhaps by a metropolitan unit of government. The determination of these specific services of a metropolitan character, as distinguished from those that are purely local, should be based upon the degree to which each may affect the residents of other municipalities in the area. The condition of purely local streets, for example, is of little concern to the total urban community; the decision to improve these streets is a matter of only localized interest. But the location and condition of major arteries are of much wider concern, having an impact upon an area much larger than the municipality in which the highway is located.

It was further suggested that instead of, or at least in addition to, placing so much emphasis upon effecting a horizantal integration of local services at the metropolitan level, attention should be directed toward developing a rational pattern for the vertical integration of urban area services provided by the federal government, the state, the county, and the municipality.

Part Three

The Nature of Urban Planning and Planning Education

Introduction

The Nature of Urban Planning and Planning Education

Differing views as to the appropriate approach to the education of city planners can be expected to follow from differing images of what city planners will be doing and should be doing in the next generation. This is apparent in the papers grouped in Part Two of this volume and emerges even more strongly in this section.

As long as the functions and form of urban planning are themselves undergoing change, and without a clearly discernible direction, there is substantial scope for controversy concerning the logical approach to planning education.

In the introduction to Part Two, it was suggested that as many as five different types of planning activities may develop in the larger urban communities, including executive staff planning, comprehensive physical planning, general socio-economic planning, and functional planning and project planning for the various public services. There are important beginnings in all of these. What seems to have been happening is that the demand for all these types of planning has been bubbling up to the surface in the bigger cities, but in an amorphous and unlabeled form. New planning and "coordinating" offices have been created in experimental fashion: the city redevelopment and renewal coordinator, the city "administrator," the mayor's adviser on planning and development matters, and the like. Project planning and functional planning have been expanding in scope, and there are beginnings in regard to socio-economic planning, for example, in connection with "area development" efforts. This growing demand has, in a sense, created a vocational vacuum, and some persons in the city planning field have come to see this as an opportunity for new and exciting activities. They, in effect, urge that the city planning profession move into this vacuum by training persons who can do well in the new planning activities, and who will, therefore, be sought after.

The greatest planning gap which has come to the forefront is that with regard to over-all executive staff planning, that is, planning concerned with all activities of a local government (their coordination, a balance among them, proper scheduling, etc.) and in close relationship to the chief executive. Those who have been concerned with problems of politics and public administration have been particularly aware of this gap and have come to put major emphasis on the requirements of this type of planning. This is where the emphasis on decision-making, communications, and "political reality" comes from, and this gets translated into suggestions that these should play a large role in the training of city planners.

Others have come to be most impressed with the gap in regard to planning for socio-economic matters—for example, the human factors in slums as against the purely physical factors, or planning to enhance the future economic health of the community. Concerns of this type have, in some cases, been translated into a broad conception of city planning and the notion that city planners should be trained chiefly in the social sciences so they can contribute importantly to the urban communities' struggles with these (priority) problems.

In summary, then, what is known as city planning has developed in the United States as an activity concerned with the physical, three-dimensional urban environment. However, persons trained as city planners, as well as others, have begun to move into the vocational vacuum created by the demand for a variety of types of planning within our larger urban communities. The question for the planning schools is this, simply: should they continue to train physical planners—surely with broad training, a sense of the complexity of the modern urban community, problem-solving-oriented, and the rest of it, but still physical planners? Or should they seek to train persons who can fill any of the planning posts within our urban communities, including not only the physical planning positions, but the other categories as well?

The problems, the opportunities, the decisions to be made, are all highlighted by the papers which are brought together in this section. None of this falls neatly into the framework suggested in the introductory notes, but the key questions emerge forcefully and many valuable insights are provided by the essays. They should make interesting reading for anyone concerned with the future of urban planning in the United States.

Chapter Nine

City Planning as a Social Movement, a Governmental Function, and a Technical Profession

by John T. Howard

Head, Department of City and Regional Planning, Massachusetts
Institute of Technology

City planning as I define it is the guidance of the growth
and change of urban areas—towns, cities, metropolitan
regions. As such, it is aimed at fulfilling certain social
and economic objectives which go beyond the physical
form and arrangement of buildings, streets and parks,
utilities, and the other component parts of the physical
urban environment. It takes effect largely through the
operations of government. It requires the application of
specialized techniques of survey, analysis, forecasting,
and design.

City planning may be characterized as a social movement, as a governmental function, or as a technical profession. Each has its own concepts, its own history, and
its own theories. Since we are concerned chiefly with the
question of training for future members of this technical profession, my principal remarks will relate to that
aspect of planning. But, together, these three ways of

looking at it fuse into the efforts of modern society to shape and improve the environment within which increasing proportions of the population not only of the country, but of the world, spend their lives—the city.

The *focus* of the technical profession must be clearly understood as the physical form of urban and metropolitan environment. It is obviously concerned with the forces that shape the environment: physical, technological, social, economic; with evaluating the environment as it now exists in terms of its capacity to satisfy human needs; and with direct and indirect consequences of planned changes. The planner is also concerned with ways of bringing into being plans for environmental improvement—and with the political implementation of these plans. But the plans themselves are plans of physical things.

History of Modern Planning

Examining briefly what I have labeled, perhaps a little sententiously, the planning movement, we might note first that it can trace at least some of its origins to the demands for social reform (that we tend to associate with Dickens' novels on slum conditions in England and housing reform) at the beginning of the past century. Various other threads from the nineteenth century are: the recreation movement, which expressed itself both in the large parks and natural reservations development and in the idea of carving out playgrounds in congested areas. We are all familiar with effects of the World's Fair of 1893 upon attitudes toward the city, and the start of what has been known, rather sneeringly, as the City Beautiful—sneeringly, because this concern with the appearance of the city seemed to some people to be a concern *only* with the appearance of the city. (I don't think this is a just appraisal, but as of now, it seems to

151

be about all that is left over of a direction of concern about the urban environment which for a while was the focus of attention of the planning movement.)

Then came, early in this century, a development of congested downtown construction. Probably if there was one technological feature that was most responsible, it was the evolution of structural steel for building. But transportation technology in the form of rapid transit facilities also had its bearing on intensive (and mixed up) growth in the middles of cities. This development brought about a feeling of the need to sort out incompatible activities and to set some limits on height and density. This in turn produced the zoning movement, which was another facet of the planning movement; 1916 is the date of the first comprehensive zoning code in New York City. Then came the automobile, adding a new kind of congestion to what was already present in the central areas. During the 1920's, perhaps the most important single concern of city planning was traffic congestion, traffic improvement, and thoroughfare plans. The depression brought a lot of people up short, with an awareness that all was not as it should be also in the areas of economic and social relations.

Somewhere along in the 1930's, there came to be crystallized, if not verbalized, a concept of the function of city planning in society as an attack upon all of these problems of the physical environment, so that in the course of the time since then, city planning has been evolving, aimed not at any single problem or reform, but at the comprehensive improvement of all aspects of the urban environment. And one of the key concepts of this approach is that all of these problems are interrelated, that no one of them can be successfully attacked in isolation.

Social Goals of Planning

The ultimate goals are clearly social, although the plans themselves are related to physical things and physical places. And the plans and the changes are also heavily concerned with intermediate economic objectives, which affect the creation, distribution, and enjoyment of wealth. The expression of these goals or objectives of planning is probably the most significant element in any discussion of planning as a movement. This is what society is asking for, from the technical profession of planning and from the governmental operation of planning machinery. And these goals have never been too clearly formulated. I have tried to abstract some which would apply more or less generally to city planning in those parts of this country where it has been taken seriously. I think we would have to agree, to begin with, on one overriding objective: that the ideal urban environment should reconcile the maximum opportunity for individual choice, in living and working and whatever else is done, with the protection of the individual from the adverse effects caused by the action of others.

Within this broad framework, I suggest the following: First would be the arrangement of functional parts of the city—residence, commerce, industry, etc.— so that each part can perform its functions with minimum cost and conflict. I would note that this goes beyond pure mechanical operation. For instance, *recognition* is necessary: each functional element needs to be visually identified in relation to the other parts of a city. (You need to know when you're in the business area and be able to find your way around. This sounds kindergarten, but it isn't.) Beyond this, another of the characteristics which society asks of our physical environment is that it be not only functional in the sense of working, but

153

that it also be comfortable and pleasant, that it have amenity, and that it provide opportunities for visual enjoyment. (For example, a trip from home to work is not a successful operation, in terms of city planning objectives, if it is merely quick and cheap. It needs also to be comfortable and pleasant. Anything less than that and we have a failure of our urban environment to achieve a basic objective.)

Second would be the linking of all parts of the city to each other and to the outside world by an efficient system of circulation. Third, the development of each part of the city according to sensible standards—for lot size, for sunlight, for green space in residential areas, for parking in business areas. Fourth, the provision of housing that is safe, sanitary, comfortable, and pleasant—in a variety of dwelling types, to meet the varied needs of all of the kinds and sizes of families, in all of their varieties of different desires. Fifth, the provision of recreation and schools and other community services of a high standard of size, location, and quality. And sixth, the provision of water supply, sewerage, and other utility and public services, adequately and economically.

This has been a statement of *general* goals of planning that would be applicable in practically any community in this country. In any particular community, there will be special goals: perhaps the preservation of a certain historic area, perhaps the protection of property values, perhaps the efficient conduct of government which is impaired by some physical feature. Sometimes these goals are inconsistent with each other, such as the elimination of substandard housing with the preservation of all property values, including property values in the slums.

But there is one other feature of these goals that I would like to stress before I leave the discussion of "movement" because it has a bearing on the technical profession. Any statement of goals requires the use of expressions like "adequate," "high standard," "optimum," "pleasant," "comfortable"; these are all relative, they are not absolute. They change from time to time. So something that is inherent in our present concept of planning is the recognition that an "ideal" is not a fixed objective, but is itself always changing and always will change; that the ideal city can be striven toward, but it can never be achieved. By the time you get close to what was your ideal the day before yesterday, you now have a new ideal. I think you can see what this means as to the nature of the plans themselves that are being dealt with.

City Planning as a Government Function

City planning as a government function, as an identifiable part of the duties of municipal government, goes back fifty years and not much more—in this country and in Europe, too. The germ of the concept of city planning as a government function is the coordination of all governmental activities that bear upon community growth and change, especially those that influence or regulate private development of all kinds, so that they all work in the direction of preconceived comprehensive objectives. The fabric of a city is made up largely of its private development, its houses and stores and factories, the private land uses, and what individual people, as citizens, do with their time. The most important decisions are the sum total of the decisions of private individuals on building or not building this, that, or the other in some location or other; so that the most important single aspect of implementing city planning, which is concerned with this whole fabric of development, is the influencing, the guiding, to some extent the controlling, of what happens to private property. Parallel with this are the developmental decisions which are within the province of government itself: streets, public parking lots, schools, parks, the other public works aspect of the urban environment. Here, too, the city planning concept is that as each of these decisions comes along, the long view, the comprehensive view, has a chance to be brought to bear to influence it—whether the action is by the city council, the city manager or mayor, the school board, or county highway department.

At the start of city planning as a government function in this country, the emphasis was on the preparation of a single, authoritative, and long-range comprehensive plan. We have been getting away from that a little, though realizing that the future is not precisely predictable so that the long-range plan has to be flexible; and also realizing that the *details* of this overview of the city are not going to be carried into effect under the "design eye" of the city planning agency. The ultimate designer is going to be the city engineer or the state highway department, or an architect hired by the school board, or the people who design business buildings, industrial buildings, residential buildings. Thus, increasingly in government operation, emphasis has come to be placed upon *planning* rather than upon the *plan;* and upon the administrative arrangements that are needed to bring this long-range and comprehensive study and review continuously to bear on applicable governmental or private decision.

In this country, with our tradition of a tripartite government structure, it is clear that public decisions of importance to community development are made both by the executive branch and by the legislative branch of municipal government. Indeed, the decisions that are of the most concern to city planning are, in form at least, made by the legislative body, not by the executive: the passage of a zoning ordinance, the adoption of standards for subdivision regulation, these key features of control over private development are legislative functions, as is the making available of funds for capital expenditures. The decisions of land acquisition and land disposition are generally legislative decisions. As city and other levels of government have evolved, however, the executive, particularly under the manager form, has been pulled into the position of taking more and more of a part in formulation of policy in areas that are ultimately responsibilities of the legislative body.

When planning was first set up as a part of municipal government, it was set up so as not to impinge on the authority of either the executive or the legislative branch, as a separate board or commission advisory to both of them—not independent, but separate. And it had no authority beyond the right to be consulted before either mayor or council acted on any matter which affected the plans. There has been a recent trend toward making planning a staff arm of the executive branch and taking away its direct access to the legislative body. (This is a trend the wisdom of which is arguable.)

As our municipal government has become more complicated, there has also been a trend toward formalizing the planning of administrative operations: budgeting, personnel work, other executive functions. This *is* properly (under the dictionary meaning of the word) planning, but has led to some confusion between these very essential kinds of planning, and city planning as the city planning profession identifies its own role—namely, a central concern with the physical environment. I am not at all sure that this confusion does not lie behind some of the recommendations from some of the top figures in public administration for rearranging relationships between the planning agency and the other elements of government.

Governmental Tools of Plan Effectuation

With the above as an overview of the relationship of planning to municipal government, it will be a further help to the understanding of the functions and activities of the technical profession to review quickly the tools of plan effectuation through operations of government.

Zoning is probably the most significant of these; certainly it is the most important historically. The regulation of use of land and buildings, the density of population, the bulk of buildings, the spaces between them—this in fact had its beginning well before the development of modern city planning. It has evolved, it has broadened its objectives, it has developed new techniques, and in general has become a more precise and more sensitive tool of regulation. It has benefited by successively broader court interpretations of the application of the police power to this kind of matter. And it is more and more being used, positively, to try to give legal effect to comprehensive plans and planning policies, rather than just negatively (as to say "you can't do that here").

Paralleling the evolution of zoning has been the evolution of subdivision controls, subjecting to review by a governmental body the initial urbanizing process of laying out lots and streets on what was formerly vacant land. Finally it has been realized, after some very bitter experience in the 1920's, that the interest of the owner of raw land is purely temporary and purely financial, while the urban community has to live forever after with whatever it is that he does to that land in turning it from country into city. The nature of the long-term public interest has finally been realized to the point where it is now an accepted procedure for municipal government to impose a very substantial degree of regulation on the process of making empty land into a part of the urban environment. This extends to requiring the developer to pay a good deal of the cost of putting in the public improvements (which, once it is developed, gives the land its value): the cost of the new streets, the cost of sidewalks, even the cost of a certain amount of land for playgrounds and schools.

Now, zoning and subdivision control, if they are carefully used (and they haven't always been), do seem to offer adequate controls over the growth of the new parts of cities—so long as there is a governmental instrumentality in existence with the authority to use them. (In much of our suburban area, this is not the case.) These regulations of private development, however, are obviously not capable of correcting past mistakes, especially to bring about the rebuilding of obsolete parts of cities.

The first step, in recognition of the need for further governmental intervention into the situation, was slum clearance for public housing—publicly owned and publicly subsidized housing. This became government policy in the United States, on a bipartisan basis, in the 1930's. Much earlier came another significant development, the new-towns movement—largely European in terms of city-building by government action. This concept, dating back to Ebenezer Howard, in the 1890's, has had a good bit of influence in this country—for instance, Kingsport, Tennessee, a new city built by industrial interests. It also had much influence on suburban real estate developments, which however (up until Park Forest) have never been really complete communities; they have been merely dormitories. But their layout was substantially influenced by the garden city idea. We did have one governmental experiment in the thirties, when the federal government undertook to build some new towns. They also never turned out to be complete. These were the "Green Belt Towns," of which there were three, all examples of good urban design, relating various kinds of housing, under a preplanned community design. This technical evolution, though essentially abortive seen in terms of governmental operations, is still stimulating and deeply concerns the profession.

To go back to the problems of rebuilding the obsolete parts of our cities: twenty years ago, there began an increasing concern with the problem of rebuilding obsolete areas. This came to the point of action with the Housing Act of 1949, again bipartisan (with Robert Taft's name on the bill), to extend the public powers of eminent domain, with the federal funds to assist in the use of these powers. The clearing of slums in blighted areas came to be seen as not just for a public reuse, but for any reuse, whether private housing or private industry or a public park or public housing, or a new railroad station, or an express highway right of way—whatever turned out to be needed in such an area viewed in terms of a long-range, large-scale picture. In the 1950's, this "urban redevelopment" became expanded as a concept into what is now called "urban renewal," which includes, in addition to wholesale clearance, the application in a systematic way of all of the powers of municipal government to the correction and prevention of blight: correction through rehabilitation, rather than through a complete clearance, as well as prevention through "conservation" measures.

This nearly completes the list of implements of planning that have been used and developed as parts of the governmental tool kit for the influencing of private land development. There is one other important instrument whose primary function is to bring planning advice to bear on the public works aspect of city development. This is the capital improvement program, a feature of administration at the municipal level which is more and more a normal part of the working of city government and is normally a function assigned to the planning agency. This is a schedule of expenditures for capital purposes—a program which is at the same time a fiscal scheduling related to the capacity of the community to pay for these things and a physical schedule for the geographical interrelationship of these projects. Such programs serve to carry further the long-range improvement goals in the comprehensive plan.

I do not want to get off onto the problems of planning jurisdictions—as between municipalities, their suburbs, and metropolitan areas—except to indicate that this is an area where planning as a governmental operation is as yet little developed. The problem is that of evolving an approach to governmental operations which will permit the reconciling of the interests of the entire metropolitan community with the legitimate separate interests, sometimes in conflict, of the much smaller groups which compose cities, towns, villages, and neighborhoods within the metropolitan area. In this regard, we should consider the possibility that the movement for metropolitan government is obsolete before it has got off the ground. What we may look to in the future is that those much maligned instruments, the state governments, will have to step in to perform the planning for the vastly expanding metropolitan areas where they are not doing it themselves; and also to exercise state powers to help implement metropolitan plans. I am quite sure this is the case in a great many of our smaller states. I would call to your attention the fact that we are concerned about the planning of metropolitan areas as they will be twenty years from now, not as they are now; and that their geographical expansion is continuous and almost explosive in the way that it proceeds in gobbling up land. At the present time, if we were to carve out any jurisdiction for metropolitan government which had any reality now, it would be tied to a piece of geography which, twenty years from now, will no longer be logical. It will be just as out of date as are the boundaries of the central city in today's metropolitan area. So, I raise a serious question as to whether we want to spend too much time in the next couple of decades sweating over machinery for metropolitan government, when perhaps what we should turn our attention to in the case of the smaller states is state environmental planning; and in the large states, the division of the states into districts, so that the entire state is covered by one district or another, with a planning operation of this kind covering each such district.

Planning as a Profession

This brings me finally to a brief discussion of planning as a technical profession. We have talked about the motivations of planning in terms of the objectives which society has set before the planners. These are the things we want to get out of planning. And we have talked about the instruments which are available now to put planning into effect through the operations of government. These have their bearing on the development of the planning profession.

Until a few decades ago, such city planning as was done was done by architects, landscape architects, or civil engineers. And in Europe today, city planning is considered to be a specialized branch of architecture. In the United States there are a few architects who believe that, because they are architects, they are also city planners; and

—if you will allow me to use such a word—fraudulently contract with unsuspecting cities and towns to undertake to perform planning services for these municipalities. There are also a few civil engineers who still claim that city planning is simply a subdivision of civil engineering and in some states have gone so far as to try through their state license boards to limit city planning to registered civil engineers. Then come the landscape architects, who are not licensed in very many states, but who point out with great logic that they, of all the older professions, are the best equipped to do city planning because they are used to dealing with space in the large rather than with individual buildings or structures like railroad lines; and that neither the city planners, the civil engineers, nor the architects should be doing this at all. In spite of all of this conflict, a group has developed which considers itself to be a separate planning profession and is so regarded quite generally.

Architecture, civil and traffic engineering (which is coming to be another specialization), geography, sociology, economics, law, all of these disciplines, and maybe more, like social psychology, all contribute to city planning. And city planners are trained to be familiar with the subject matter and the techniques of each of these fields, though they are not necessarily expert in any of these fields. But the core of the city planner's specialized professional concern is a subject matter which is not within the universal competence of any of the other or older professions. And for this, I will quote from the Constitution of the American Institute of Planners, which is our professional society. This concern is "the unified development of urban communities and their environs, as expressed through determination of the comprehensive arrangement of land uses and land occupancy, and the regulation thereof." This, I submit, is

163

something which a professional city planner has to know about, or he is not a professional city planner. It is something which a professional architect may know about, but he can be a perfectly good architect without knowing this. A specialist in public administration may have picked up this competence in the course of his activity, but a city manager can be a very good city manager without having it—and so on. This is the central focus of the planning profession; it is a focus which is not central to any other profession. And on this, we base our case for being regarded as a separate profession.

In identifying the character of this profession, there are some intriguing dangers. One of them is a consequence of the emphasis which comes in the way the planner spends his time. The functions that the planner (or the planning agency) performs involve analysis of problems, which includes making projections of what is likely to happen; goal formulation, the determination of the objectives, limited by the analysis, to realizable objectives; the design aspect, that is, the preparation of the plan to achieve these objectives; and finally, the implementation of these plans. In his operations in the field, the professional city planner spends a good deal more time and energy on steps one, two, and four, than on step three; and in steps one, two, and four, a great deal of his concern is with matters social, economic, and political. There is therefore some risk of over-emphasis of the social, economic, and political aspects of planning as a profession. But city planning is like all other operations of government in having social and economic objectives and political methods of application. (So do the operations of the city engineer, in building a sewer, or designing a bridge.) The product of the planning is physical. It must be stressed and restressed that city planning, as a profession, is a design profession. I do not mean that it is a part of architecture, any more than architecture is a part of furniture design, or either of them bears any relationship to automobile design. But it is a profession concerned with the design of cities.

As I said earlier, in terms of the function of the parts of the city, which is one of the main subject matters of the professional activity, this kind of design is concerned not solely with visual appearance, but neither is it blind to visual appearance. This brings in a special relationship between this design field of planning at the city-wide scale and with the design profession which is the closest to it, that of architecture. City planners in this country are not necessarily competent in the visual design of three-dimensional forms. And at the scale of large groups of buildings, like public housing projects or civic centers, it is also regrettably true that architects are also not necessarily competent. (Some of them are; I do not believe, however, that the percentage of architects who are good at this kind of thing is very much higher than the corresponding percentage of city planners.) This gap has become noticed at the same time that tremendous new opportunities for large-scale operations have come before us. Urban redevelopment in the inner parts of towns is one of the biggest of these. At the same time, there are the sweeping suburban developments—of industrial parks, of regional shopping centers, and of large-scale house building. There are large-scale design operations (large-scale from the point of view of the architect, small-scale from the point of view of the city planner) in connection with college and university development as they are faced with the tremendous increases in the numbers of their students over the next twenty years. Their physical expansion is going to be a major kind of opportunity for this sort of design, as will the groupings of public buildings and the revitalization of downtown business districts. All of these are opportunities that are becoming more and more real.

There seem to be too few people that know how to handle these opportunities effectively, in terms of the optimum of both mechanical functioning and visual pleasure. Some call this urban design, some call it civic design. It is either a marriage between architecture and city planning, or else it is something new that fits in between the two; I don't know that it quite matters. But the situation does indicate an opportunity for a specialized kind of training, with which educational establishments which are concerned with either architects or city planners may also be concerned.

This, however, is separate from the training of the planning professional as such. It has been urged that every "generalist" planner should also have training in a specialty, since the planning task must be a team job. Certainly the operations of a planning *agency* are going to be team operations. There are going to be people working for a large planning agency who are professionally sociologists, others who are professionally land economists, others who are professionally architects; beyond that, probably the majority of the professional positions will be in city planning. It has been said, however, that *beyond* a full-scale use of these other professions, there is a place for specialization within the planning profession. I disagree. Although it is entirely likely that planning professionals will have different bents and directions, this will probably be a consequence of undergraduate training before they entered planning education, or of previous professional education if they entered planning without a planning degree. I see no reason, however, why such specialization is desirable or necessary. In a planning school, I am sure there is enough of "generalist" material to fill up a full two years of graduate work, so that there is no possible time, in that minimum period, to move in the direction of specialization *within* the planning profession. In a Ph.D. program aimed at research or teaching, the picture is different. But at the professional level of training, the minimum for which is generally accepted as a two-year program, a curriculum which permits specialization, or encourages it or insists on it, will reduce beyond an acceptable limit that common core of things that every city planner ought to know.

A tremendous proportion of the urban planning that needs doing, and that is going to be receiving the attention of these professionals we're going to be training over the next twenty years, is going to be done in small communities, where there will be probably only one or at the most two professional planners. It is important that these be general practitioners, rather than specialists. By the same token, in a large city, once you arrive at the stage of Planning Director, the generalist is more likely to have an impartial and balanced view than the specialist.

Future Trends

The techniques of city planning, the things that city planners have to learn how to do, are in flux. City planning started as an art, with all decisions being made intuitively. It has gradually been equipped with some of the tools of science. It turns for insights into the social and economic functioning of urban communities to specialists in those fields. It turns to technology for solutions to environmental problems, such as traffic handling, or innovations in housing, or shopping center development. What the future evolution of the profession will be will depend in part on what it can learn

167

how to do and in part on what demands are placed upon it by society.

One prospect that is pushed in front of the city planners, at least once during every one of their national conventions, is that our urban and environmental planning profession may expand into a truly comprehensive planning profession whose concern is the improvement, not just of physical environment, but of society—of social and economic and political relations. I reject this. In the first place, I think it is beyond the scope of any single profession to undertake a responsibility like this. It may need doing, but if it does, it is going to involve all of the disciplines that now exist and maybe some that don't. And it is going to involve all of these disciplines, guided not only by a greater level of knowledge than we have now, but I think by a higher level of wisdom than we have yet proved able to bring to bear on problems of planning our social future. And certainly it isn't going to have some retreaded city planner as the team captain. I can think of only two kinds of people for team captain for really comprehensive planning like that: one would be the preacher, and the other would be the philosopher. It seems a little futile and definitely premature to talk in these terms about a profession which now exists with a definite job (that it isn't doing too well and is already too big for it) within its own, narrowly circumscribed limits.

For the near future, I would be content for this profession to develop by extending its competence to do its presently assigned job of planning for the urban environment—with a much more solid base than it now has from research and with stronger bridges to the related disciplines, from which the planning profession needs help that it hasn't yet been able to get in all cases (and incidentally, to which the planning field may itself be

able to make some contribution). Then for the intermediate future, a little beyond the immediate, I can
see the need for extending the techniques of our concern with the physical environment, and the scope of
environmental planning and our competence to perform it, to larger-scale regions than the urban metropolitan region. (We are not complete strangers to gestures
in this direction, such as the TVA; but this large a scale
regional planning is a professional area of activity
which is still to be grown into.) Certainly this is going
to be necessary, if any of the projections of future population for the world are to be taken seriously, coupled as
they must be with the fact that a larger and larger proportion of world population is living under urban circumstances. Certainly we are going to have to find ways
of ordering and organizing our physical environment
to make this globe tolerable, until the point when we
can either colonize the planets of some far flung star, or
find some other answer to the unchecked increase in
the numbers of our population.

Theory ought to underlie practice. Planning theory
in terms of understanding the past and the present is
still underequipped with scientific knowledge. Research
is needed; it is being begun on a large scale. But there
is a lot more that we can see to be necessary than can
be undertaken with the present resources. Planning
theory in terms of identifying more nearly ideal forms
for the urban environment of the future is also underequipped, both with scientific knowledge of what people will need in the future (and for this, we turn,
I suppose, not only to the social sciences, but to the
natural sciences in the area of technology), but also, with
prophetic insight as to what people will want in terms
of the shape of the environment. We had Ebenezer
Howard in the 1890's; we have had some visions by

169

Le Corbusier and by Frank Lloyd Wright, two architects. We have had visions from Patrick Geddes, a zoolgist. It is high time we had some more of this kind of prophesying.

These are the challenges to city planning (and to all of the related professional disciplines) that we face, and they are also the challenges that anybody faces who sets out to train members for this profession.

Comments by Robert C. Weinberg

Consultant on City Planning, New York University

1. *In training planners to design future urban areas, we must get them to think about what living will be like in times to come and what people will want under new circumstances.*

As important as it is for planners to know how to meet the continuing demands of immediate and short-term problems based on present-day living habits (many of them already on the way out), their fundamental training must be with respect to anticipating future needs rather than simply satisfying present ones.

We want to train planners to think about what people want the cities of the future to be like, insofar as there may be (and increasingly are) opportunities to design them from scratch. Whether it is clearing the forest for an industrial center to smelt aluminum in Canada or draining a swamp to establish a modern city in one of the great new nations in Asia or Africa, we've got to

171

think of what cities are going to be in the future. Even though patching up what's been handed us, difficult as that is, may be what is more often demanded of planners at home and in the immediate future, their training should be oriented to the more creative, positive side of civic design. This is how I interpret Mr. Howard's final statement about a prophetic insight into what people would want in the future.

2. *The planner must develop confidence in his own design judgment.*

The professional planner should have confidence in his own judgment in the field in which he is expert and submit his plans and his designs without compromise or concession to the desires and tastes of lay pressure groups whether these be lawyers, bankers, politicians, real estate men, or sentimentalists, and (this is most important of all), the general public, including small property owners who may be inconvenienced. The well-trained planner, respecting his own intellectual and artistic integrity and taking into account, only to the extent that his knowledge and training tells him he should, the criticisms and strictures he may anticipate from these various sources, must be expected to prepare his plans forthrightly and courageously and let the responsibility for rejection or compromise fall entirely on the elected or appointed officials who have the final legal say in the matter.

I do not mean to imply, lest anyone should thus interpret it, that the staff members of a large planning agency in a big city should be permitted to issue separate statements to the public; far from it, for this would only lead to confusion. I do mean that whoever is responsible for an expert answer to any given planning question, whether it is the appointed planning agency, the retained planning consultant, or the specially established *ad hoc* board of review—any one of which is presumably chosen on the ground of competence in the planning field—should be listened to and respected because of that competence rather than expected to compromise *in advance,* or negotiate as a *technical equal,* with the representatives of law, administration, finance, business, or individual ownership.

There has been too great a tendency in this country to let laymen, whether they are members of planning commissions (where their functions are important in deciding general over-all city policy) or members of *so-called* boards of review, make decisions as to what constitutes a good design, and this refers to both the esthetic and the technical aspects of that design. Even if it is judged that planning as a design profession is still in its infancy in this country, the people we are training for that profession should, nevertheless, logically expect to be called upon as the arbiters of good esthetic as well as technical design. The citizen members of the planning commission will increasingly rely on these specialists for such decisions. For instance, you don't expect a board of health that is made up of laymen to formulate the medical regulations needed to deal with an epidemic; you expect them to consult the physicians for that.

Actually, it isn't a question of what the public may want. It's a question of what is good urban design and environment *in the opinion of those who have been trained to create a new sort of environment out of the conditions they have to work with.* For the man who may want to climb mountains with a weak heart, it is not a question of what *he wants* to do, but of following the advice of his physician who may say that, since he has a cardiac condition, he can't climb the mountain without risking his life, but he could very possibly

173

become an expert bowler. Like the physician, who respects his professional dignity, the urban designer must stand on his own feet and be prepared to take the responsibility for his decisions and advice. This is something that has always been accorded to the professional designer abroad; but we tend, to some extent, to confuse such respect (when we come across it in Germany, France, Switzerland or Scandinavia) with a lack of what we call "democratic principles." We sometimes think it is "authoritarian"—comparable to dictating a political, financial, or administrative decision without popular referendum—to render, a scientific, technical, and esthetic opinion that is based on training and knowledge. This is not so. Such decisions, I feel, should *not* be left to people who have not been trained for that purpose. And I believe that we can, and should, look forward to training planners to have full respect for their professional competence in this field, and to expect them to be treated as experts who lead the way and not mere employees who submit to the prejudices of uninformed nonprofessionals.

3. *With our involvement with ever growing urban areas leading us to a proper concern about metropolitan and regional planning, we may be losing sight of the equally important need of breaking down our biggest cities into smaller community units, for administrative as well as for planning purposes.*

When Mr. Howard was speaking about the fact that the larger framework of planning may not, in the future, be even the metropolis but the *state* (or a district of the state), I was reminded that we ought—at the same time—consider the opposite end of the scale, the smaller subdivision of government as a planning unit. In our big cities we have lost sight of the community that is of human size. Incidentally, this is something that Mr.

Howard is well aware of. In Cleveland, a decade or two ago, he showed how *within* that city, which was then just under a million in population, there were a dozen or more distinct communities. The planners were called upon to plan those communities individually in respect to matters which did *not* have city-wide, much less county-wide or region-wide, significance. When it came to such matters as the location of a playground, or where a cluster of neighborhood stores should go, or on which local streets you ought to allow trucks to travel and where not, plans could not be made on the level of a vast metropolis, but only at the local level. Within our great cities these local problems can be solved with the assistance, on the one hand, of citizen groups who know intimately those areas of the city; and, on the other hand, by technical planners on the staff of the planning agency *who have been specially assigned over a continuing period* to study that particular community or area.

It seems to be taken for granted in many planning agencies that it is enough to study the big city as a whole; then, if there arise problems peculiar to one or another special section of the vast city, to send someone to spend a day or two looking at it and come out with the answer. This shows not only a poor conception of community planning but displays a less than decent respect for human values. To the individual community *within* our great cities the intimate things that concern it are as important as the city-wide policies. They call for close and *continuous* collaboration between, on the one hand, the local people (who know intimately every street and every corner and every institution, every saloon, every church, every dangerous crossing, every housing violation, every tree worth keeping and every favorite bird perch, or what have you); and, on the

175

other hand, the trained planner from the planning agency's staff who should be assigned to the local community *over a long period of time* so that he can become familiar with it. To think in terms of the community within the city is as serious a part of the planner's task as to set his sights in the opposite direction and to think only of the big problems in terms of metropolitan or state regions or even larger frameworks.

4. *The tendency toward larger and larger areas of planning concern is leading us also to forget the more precise and intimate problems of true urban design and human amenities and scale in our distinctly urban areas.*

With the architects becoming more and more preoccupied with the highly specialized aspects of their profession—the structure and mechanical equipment, as well as school, apartment, hospital, theater, and other special building types—they are even less concerned than they may have been in the past with the relationship of one building to another and the effect of the bulk, shape, and color of their structures to the surrounding neighborhood in respect to the movement of people and vehicles, to open space, and to aesthetic composition. They leave all of this to the planning profession which, in the mind of the average busy, highly specialized architect of today appears vaguely as a new group of specialists that will relieve him of all responsibility and concern for anything outside of the four walls of his building. The planner, at the same time, is going further and further afield—physically toward city-wide and now region-wide areas while, theoretically, he is wandering way off center from urban design toward more and more abstruse aspects of sociology, engineering, and economics, to say nothing of such peripheral specialties

176

as economic geography, traffic control, industrial location, and so forth.

In this doubly centrifugal dispersion of the architectural and planning professions, a vacuum is being created in the middle. The true heart of the planning technique is left out in the cold with no one concerned about it. It is high time that the planning profession remember that this is where they came in originally; and intriguing and even important as the study and practice of these newer, but peripheral, aspects of planning may be, planners must not lose sight of the central importance of true civic design as the core of planning practice and consequently of the training of planners.

5. *A final point: we must train planners to recognize and design for the character of an urban area of whatever size.*

The planner need not necessarily know whether buildings in a housing group should be sixteen stories high or twenty stories high or whether they should be forty feet apart, or set back twenty-five feet from the street-line; but he should know something about, and *say* something about, the *character* a project should have. Now, the character of an area is a subtle thing. For example, take Greenwich Village or Brooklyn Heights in New York. These are two communities, both *within* a large city, whose chief character is a certain small-scale intimacy—which is the result, to some extent, of a pattern of narrow, irregular streets inherited from the eighteenth and the early nineteenth century. They encourage more pedestrian than vehicular use, and suggest small, specialized shops and individual townhouses rather than supermarkets, detached "homes" or high-rise apartments. To recogize the *character* of such communities, so that whatever is designed in the way of new developments is appropriate, is more important for the

177

planner than the technicalities of setbacks, or angles of sunlight, and a lot of other things which the architect can worry about. The planner should be trained (whether his background is in architecture or in sociology) to recognize the *character* of the community for which he is working. Obviously, a small New England village has an entirely different character from a city on the plains in Kansas or an eighteenth-century downtown district in an eastern seaboard metropolis. But all the more subtle differences in urban *character* should be taught in our schools and our planners trained in ways of designing for them in a physical sense as well as in a social sense.

Chapter Ten

Urban Design and City Planning

by G. Holmes Perkins
Dean, School of Fine Arts, University of Pennsylvania

City planning is directed to the ultimate creation of homes, schools, highways, industrial and business centers, parks, and all the myriad elements of our environment which make life richer, easier, more productive, and more satisfactory for all. The final three-dimensional result is architecture, civic design, and landscape architecture. Without the foundation made possible through those arduous and perceptive social and economic studies which give character and dimensions to the program of development, the final stage of physical design would not be reached. Conversely without an efficient, harmonious, and beautiful design of the city and its parts as the end product, the finest surveys, analyses, and statistical projections would be wasted.

The goal of all our calculations, analyses, political actions, surveys, and designs is to create a climate in which progress can be made toward an environment

179

that will promote better living for everybody. We are, therefore, concerned with all of the elements and with all the professions which contribute to a good design. Although the design professions have, during the past century, developed a jealous independence of one another, any so-called traditional separation is not a historic fact. It is, rather, a new development—a tragic one. It is useless, however, to spend time arguing the present shortcomings of the professions which contribute to the design of cities. Our concern, instead, should be with those more positive factors which will allow us to work toward some common agreement as to how we go about getting this better environment.

Foremost is the necessity of agreement upon those social and visual values which are the conscious or unconscious basis of all designs. In architectural terms, this is a problem of form. We cannot and should not attempt to preconceive the form that the city should or will take. Over a hundred years ago Horatio Greenough warned, "We shall seek in vain, to borrow shapes. We must make the shapes and can only effect this by mastering the principles." In part, these principles are immutable laws of nature, but in major part are based upon those values which we cherish and upon which we make both ethical and practical decisions. The form of the city in the hands of the creative designer will grow naturally out of this soil. Greenough goes on to say, "If there is any principle of structure more plainly inchoate in the works of the Creator than all others, it is the principle of unflinching adaptation of forms to functions. I believe the colors also, so far as we have discovered their chemical causes and affinities, are not less organic in relation to the forms they invest than are those forms themselves."

In the design of cities which, by definition, involves

180

modification of the environment, we work within natural laws concerned with the biotic balance of nature. But in the planning process we also have many choices to make. Who makes these decisions, and the manner of their making is of vital importance. We like, as planners, to think that we make the essential decisions. This is only partly true. There are many persons and corporations whose actions, uninfluenced by the city planner, often have decisive and sometimes disastrous effects on the quality of city living. Not the least of these are the manufacturers whose cars have made and scarred our cities. High on the city planner's list of problems must be that of finding a way of making others aware of the impact of apparently unconnected acts upon the shape and the quality of the city.

Yet, far more important is the *attitude* that man takes toward his environment. Attitudes differ, not only with individuals, but with peoples and nations whose historic traditions and whose religions have fostered unique views of nature. These different attitudes are strikingly illustrated in the forms of their cities and in their architecture. In this country we are dedicated to freedom of religious thought; we take a pride in democracy. The form of the city based upon these principles will differ completely from the cities of mediaeval times or those of tyrants or of emperors, quite apart from any technological changes which will also have decisive impact upon the form. Therefore, the architectonic form of our cities will, in the last analysis, be far more an expression of the spiritual feelings of a people as interpreted by the artists of the day than a mere technological solution of a practical problem.

It is in this realm of ideas that the greatest contributions are *yet* to be made. I say this with the full knowledge that many persuasive ideas have been spawned in the past sixty years. All critics agreed on the dire shortcomings of the late nineteenth-century city and the need for surgery, but here agreement stopped. Many utopias were proposed; some experiments were made. From this ferment of ideas also came the trenchant social and historical survey and analytical methods of Geddes which included a reaffirmation of the biological basis for the pattern of human settlement. Among the utopias was the Garden City of Ebenezer Howard and that relative newcomer, the Vertical Garden City of Le Corbusier. Ideas ranging from the super-block to the regional city were pioneered and expounded most eloquently by Clarence Stein and Lewis Mumford. The competitive impact of the booming regional shopping centers upon the design of the center city is everywhere evident today. Among the many fertile ideas put forward was one quite different, but nonetheless significant, which appears in the Goodmans' *COMMUNITAS* where several plans are developed to a logical conclusion based on differing value assumptions. The importance of this work lies entirely in the method of attack rather than in the physical plans illustrated, for such methods open practical ways whereby the analyst and designer may effectively collaborate. The indivisibility of the process of program-making and designing is here convincingly demonstrated, yet we remain all too often unaware of the consequences of the values we set as a basis for decision-making. Let me illustrate.

When a community builds a school, it would like to put it in the right spot. This is seldom feasible in the judgment of the school board because of the cost of land which nearly always forces the selection of a site too small or too remote. On the assumption that there is a rational basis for choosing the right piece of land, how can we avoid the veto imposed by cost. Here again we face the question of relative values. The British overcame this dilemma by nationalizing the development rights in the land, well knowing that they were exchanging one set of problems for another. We, on the other hand, chose to pay, by way of urban redevelopment subsidies, the price necessary to make a more logical and efficient pattern of land use in our cities even though with such aid we remain under severe economic pressure to overdevelop the land.

The schools are not alone in being under such severe economic pressure that no freedom of choice remains in selecting a site. Recently in a large city, a beautiful home for the aged was built overlooking the river. It's a very lovely site but chosen less for this reason than because it was already owned by the city—lying as it does between the filtration plant and the house of correction. Its dreadful isolation raises in a new form the persistent and plaguing problems of segregation. Why should these people be cut off by an official planning decision from youth, from friends, and from relatives? There must be something wrong with our social values which not merely permit but promote such planning.

Within a democracy we place a very high value on variety. For is it not variety which alone can offer the greatest freedom of choice to the family, the individual, and the group? Only if there is variety of opportunity in work, in recreation, and in education for young and old and for those with the most diverse tastes and interests, can we provide a community where all persons, of whatever age, can maintain ties to friends and neighbors. To build such variety of choice and at the same time the promise of stability into our plans is a most difficult task, which might well become a trap for the unwary and unskilled. The concept of the vast and impersonal project—whether public or private—is the very antithesis of that small New England village whose warmth and friendliness is so beloved and in which there is to be gained a richness of experience because of the variety of people whom one meets every day. If these democratic values are to be preserved in our city plans, we must reassess the criteria upon which we make our decisions. We are increasingly free to make these choices, for we are entering that "Affluent Society" which Galbraith describes so well. The question therefore is, are we really choosing to do the right things? We have constantly increased the proportion we devote to our homes and to public amenities. These are the decisions which make your local plans.

There are also world-wide forces acting upon all cities, which as yet we do not fully understand, that will shape our future environment in ways yet undreamed. Our cities are going to become so fantastically big that the problems raised will be without precedent. Critical as this impact will be on cities in technologically advanced nations, it may well prove to be a crushing burden on the less advanced areas of the world. Growth is occurring faster than decisions can be taken and plans developed. To look backwards to avoid the mistakes of nineteenth-century England or America will not produce the dynamic new ideas, designs, and leadership which alone are capable of saving mankind from even greater squalor than the worst of Dickens' time. Even these new problems can be defined and are capable of analysis; goals can be set; from these, designs can be made; and decisions can be taken which can lead to effective action. This is the indivisible essence of city and metropolitan planning, the end product of which is a better physical environment.

As you can see, we demand a great deal of this new profession of planning. (Defined in this way, it is truly new.) We ask a single individual to comprehend the aspirations of other individuals, groups, and whole communities, to have the skills to measure the needs and the resources, to understand the power of history and the social, economic, and political forces within a city, to produce designs which "will stir men's souls," and to devise the means to reach the goals. The skills required are cetrainly not to be found in any one existing profession, and it is surely presumptuous to imagine that the future planner will ever be able to compete as a specialist with the social scientist, architect, lawyer, and administrator. His specialty is none of these though his earlier education may, to his advantage, have been in one of these professions. His contribution will lie rather in his ability to give due weight to all elements of the planning process and to utilize with consummate diplomacy the precious skills of all the specialists. In his education, therefore, he must gain an understanding of the contributions of all to city planning. Nor is mere secondhand knowledge in any way an effective substitute for firsthand contact with the job whether it be in the survey, analysis, administrative, or design aspects of this basically indivisible process of planning and decision-making.

In his "Affluent Society" Galbraith suggests that our problem lies not in our ability to produce whatever we want but rather in our inability to choose what we want. Upon this point I am in complete agreement, even though in some parts of the world production at this level of affluence may not be reached for another generation or two, the problem is only one of time. Successful planning depends upon the skill with which choices can be placed before those who make the decisions, and in a democratic society this group should be as large as we can make it. Yet if we are to make progress, we must

185

experiment with plans for which we find no precedent. To ask people to make choices between knowns and unknowns raises enormous problems for the planner who must present in attractive and yet realistic terms the improvements which he has visualized. Single improvements and scattered projects are easy to sell, as witness the staggering outlay for federal highways or the big city political support for slum clearance. To achieve a reasonable balance in the expenditure of public funds through the planning process is the hardest task of all. Yet perhaps one harder task remains, which is to convince our present social scientists, our architects, or our administrators that their truly collaborative efforts are needed, and that no one of them (with their present professional attitudes) can produce the city plan without the collaboration of all the others. If the new profession of city planning is to grow to its fullest stature, it will require a more sympathetic attitude of mind among its older professional brothers. This growth of a new profession is inevitable; it is desirable; and the sooner all the older professions lend support to the newcomer, the sooner we may enjoy the fruits of an improved environment.

From the series of decisions will come the new city whose form will follow no preconceived ideas of architect or politician but will develop a new shape and beauty as natural to our society as were all cities of the past to theirs. It will possess variety and order, for we will insist on the richest range of choice of home, of work, of recreation, and of education. The city will grow with a will of its own as a direct result of these social decisions and of our technology; its expressive form will depend upon the creative genius of its architects. Its organic beauty will be as inevitable as that of the clipper ship so lovingly described by Greenough: "Observe a ship at sea, mark the majestic form of her hull as she rushes through the water, observe the graceful bend of her body, the gentle transition of round to flat, the grasp of her keel, the leap of her bows, the symmetry and the rich tracery of her spars and rigging and those grand wind muscles, her sails."

Chapter Eleven

Decision Making and Planning

by Herbert Simon
Graduate School of Industrial Administration, Carnegie Institute of Technology

In the construction and organization of a city, as in the design and organizing of industries into a coordinated economy, it is possible to fit individual decisions together to create a pattern through a highly decentralized decision-making process. This process relies largely on individuals pursuing their own interests to make the component decisions. We know that in some areas of human activity this is a satisfactory method of doing business.

The mere fact that something has gotten itself organized does not mean that it is necessarily good or that we like the organization that has resulted; however, anything we propose to do about the city, any way which we propose to modify the design has to be accomplished against the background of a highly decentralized decision-making system. We are not in the position where there are just a few dials which control the planning process. The planner is playing a far more complicated game than the architect. The architect can determine the details as soon as he can get the contractor to read his blueprints and the client to agree. These are minor problems compared to the consensus goal of the urban planner.

Decentralized decision-making has further conse-quence. Whenever we make decisions through our cen-tral powers to modify the pattern of the city, the hundreds and thousands of other decision-makers, who are pursuing their own interests, will respond to the situation created by our planning decisions. For ex-ample, planners may provide new transportation facil-ities, but as a result of the new facilities, the community wants to carry out different activities because they are responding to the new facilities. People in any metro-politan area have a capacity for creating problems at least as fast as we have for solving them.

There are two difficulties of a theory of urban plan-ning which considers it a process in which you lay out a design of the city and then you take the action which will implement that design. First, nobody has really asked you to design a city. At best, they have given you certain very limited powers to modify the design. Sec-ondly, when you do intervene to modify the city, the people in that city, who control the other variables, are going to react to your decision. As a result, any adequate approach to city planning and decision-making has to substitute this kind of dynamic notion of the planning process for the notion of a static city plan or city design. This does not mean that the design does not play a role in a city planning, but it will have to play a much more complicated and sophisticated role than it has in the past.

We live in a culture in which it is appropriate to

look to the future, to think about the future, and to act today with a view to the future. I am not really disagreeing with this point of view, but I am saying that the only decisions we really make, ought to make, or ought to be worried about making, are the decisions for what we are going to do *now*. When we plan for a city, I think we have to ask how far we want to carry our visualization of the future. There are many things about the future that are completely irrelevant in the present. I do not mean that all decisions are only decisions for the present. There are certain decisions that are either absolutely or relatively irrevocable. Many of the decisions with which city planners are concerned have a certain irrevocability about them. One of the reasons why planning activities tend to be preoccupied with the physical aspects of the plan is that the decisions we make about the physical plan are the least reversible parts of the plan.

I do not want to overemphasize the relation between the need for looking toward the future and the tangibility of the things about which you make your decisions, but in our planning efforts we need to make some decisions about our planning horizon. One of the criticisms that can be directed against the master planning activity of the past is that planners expended a great deal of energy predicting and estimating things that really didn't have any bearing on what actual projects were to be undertaken in the future. Ordinarily, the amount of effort we have available for planning is not unlimited. As a result it is necessary to be sophisticated about the things that we carry out to the fourth decimal place.

I can provide a striking example of this point from a field quite separate from city planning. Since before World War I, the United States military departments have been prepared for every war with a set of rather complete mobilization plans. In the two World Wars, these mobilization plans were largely unused because the plans were conceived as specific and definite patterns of activity which would be undertaken in an emergency. If you ask yourself what kind of a mobilization plan would be likely to have influence on governmental action during an emergency, I think you would conclude that the plan should explore the central issues of organizing a nation for a wartime economy, should digest out of this analysis some basic principles about methodology, and should attempt to train a large number of people to understand these principles with the hope that some of them would be among those who would do the actual organizing and planning during a subsequent emergency.

In contrast to mobilization for war, city planning, and the execution of city planning, is not normally accomplished under emergency planning pressures, but is accomplished with the participation of a large number of people of whom the professionals are only a small fraction. Planning is completed with the enlistment of extensive public support and understanding; therefore, the preparation of detailed and specific plans constitutes only a small part of the planning effort. A large part of planning must be devoted to the determination of a few guiding principles and the dissemination of these principles to key figures who may be involved in providing a basis of public support and public understanding for the implementation of the plan. In the past, we have been more successful in learning how to create detailed plans than in learning how to communicate some of the basic objectives and goals to influential members of the community with the expectation that if they understood the goals, the eventual product would be reasonable and desirable.

The professional decision-maker, in city planning or in any field where he is in the role of technical adviser to a consumer, is in a position where, through his planning and projecting activities, he can propose alternatives. He can suggest new ways of building a city. He doesn't simply select out of a kit of existing designs the one that he thinks is going to be the best for the city. His job is to formulate alternatives which have not been proposed previously. Any theory of decision-making, which would be relevant to the city planning process, would have to insure that alternatives are generated, so that the professional planners and the opinion leaders could decide among meaningful alternatives.

Social science theories of decision-making have been weak and inadequate in failing to recognize the very large role that has to be played by the professional planner in creating images of cities for the contemplation and consideration of the opinion leaders who must make decisions related to the selected image.

In closing, I would like to refer to the development of technical procedures in the decision-making art which has occurred in the past decade. These techniques promise to contribute a great deal to the power of the designer in any complicated field. For example, operations research techniques have been applied to the design of highways and to problems of traffic congestion. Operations research enlarges the range of technical matters that the planner can encompass in his plan and the complexity of the situation with which he must deal, but I do not think that the new techniques will fundamentally affect the relationship between the decision-making process and city planning.

Comments by Glenn W. Ferguson

Associate, McKinsey and Company, Inc.
Washington, D.C.

Initially, we should recognize that the word "planning" is used in a dual sense. In the first place, we refer to planning as a profession in which the concept of planning becomes an end in itself. Planning, in this context, is a function of government for which there are tangible manifestations of progress.

In the second place, "planning" is considered an integral step in the process of administration. When a decision is made, it must be "planned" or programmed, controlled, and eventually reappraised. When "planning" is used in the sense, we are discussing one vital aspect of the process of administration with which every administrator, including the planner, is concerned. Today, we shall discuss the elements of decision-making, the first step in the process of administration, in relation to the planning profession.

The typical planning practitioner does not have

sufficient time or interest to investigate the basic theoretical materials dealing with decision-making in administration. It is true that these materials are generally obscured in academic journals, but it is unfortunate that planners do not possess sufficient motivation to test the applicability of decision-making models in an operational ecology.

The leading authors in decision-making theory state that there are several distinct elements in the decision-making process. Chester Barnard lists means, ends, and conditions as the requisite components of decision-making. Tannenbaum and Massarik define decision-making as the "conscious choice or selection of one behavior alternative from among a group of two or more behavior alternatives." Peter Drucker presents a five-step analysis: defining the problem, analyzing the problem, developing alternate solutions, deciding upon the best solution, and converting the decision into effective action. The final step in this analysis confuses the decision-making and planning phases of the process of administration, but the breakdown demonstrates the traditional view of decision-making.

Herbert Simon suggests that when you adopt the Barnardian dichotomy of means and ends, factual judgments and value judgments are confused. Dr. Simon defines factual judgments as decisions regarding the implementation of values and value judgments as decisions in which you select final goals. Armed with this refinement of terms, Dr. Simon presents a three-fold analysis of decision-making: isolating alternative strategies, determining the consequences of each of the alternatives, and evaluating, comparatively, the sets of consequences.

Recently, Edward H. Litchfield has suggested that decision-making involves the following subactivities:

definition of the issue, analysis of the existing situation, calculation and delineation of alternatives, deliberation, and choice. To complete the spectrum of theoretical decision-making, we should mention the integration of a prediction system and a value system as presented by Irwin Bross.

What is the practical impact of these attempts to describe the process by which we arrive at decisions? Are these authors merely engaging in academic gymnastics or will their efforts assist the planner in his operational assignment?

Traditionally, we have assumed that certain individuals are endowed with the innate ability to make "good" decisions. We have accepted the stereotype that it is not feasible to teach a potential administrator "how to make decisions," but at the same time, we are aware of the multiplicity of factors which must be considered in the contemporary decision-making process. It was possible for yesterday's planner to appraise the relatively limited number of alternatives, to react intuitively, and in the majority of cases, to render that "right" decision. In contrast, the planner of tomorrow may discover that the attributes of "good sense," intuition, and practical experience are inadequate to cope with the complexity of modern urbanism.

In the past, the planner retained his identification with one of the substantive professional fields related to the planning process. The planner was an architect, and engineer, a geographer, or a sociologist, and he approached planning from the familiar vantage point of his specialty. In this milieu, the planner was able to maintain his substantive competence, to read the current literature of his chosen field, and to approach vital decision areas with confidence and a reasonable assurance of success.

If Harvey Perloff's prognosis is correct, the planner of tomorrow will become a "generalist with a specialty." He will approach planning problems as a planner, not as a specialist, and he will be expected to appraise a mushrooming maze of confusing, complicated, conflicting, and interrelated facts and concepts before reaching a decision. He will be asked to understand the seamless web of jurisdiction, the changing mores of a dynamic urban population, the impact of mass and rapid transit, and a hundred other profundities with which the planner is hopefully more familiar than I. Time will be of the essence, the margin of excusable error will be reduced, and the planner will become the focal point upon whom more than 70 per cent of our population will depend for intelligent leadership. In this labyrinth, is it not reasonable to assume that the planner will expect and require assistance in meeting the decision-making challenge?

In *Models of Man,* Herbert Simon has stated that "the capacity of the human mind for formulating and solving complex problems is very small compared with the size of the problem whose solution is required for objectively rational behavior in the real world—or even for a reasonable approximation to such objective rationality." Dr. Simon has labeled this concept the principle of bounded rationality. For the planner, this principle implies that any theory of decision-making will be limited by the narrow boundaries of rational human behavior. Even if the planner is armed with a meaningful checklist of "steps to good decision-making," the practical limits to rationality will preclude the development of an infallible model.

Will it be possible for operations research to transcend the principle of bounded rationality? Will the theory of games, statistical decision theory, queueing theory, linear programming, and the theory of optimum distribution of effort allow the planner to approach the decision-making arena with self-confidence and impunity? According to Dr. Simon, these modern theories ignore the principle of bounded rationality. In addition, he suggests that they neglect the elements of "surprise, struggle, and relative human difficulty."

Certainly, automation and operations research techniques will not insure the planner's role as a recipient of unemployment compensation, but at the same time, we should not ignore the potential impact of operations research on the decision-making process. If the planner can be relieved of the detailed analysis which statistics and the machine are more capable of discharging, he should be better able to cope with the elements of "surprise, struggle, and relative human difficulty." Operations research may become the planner's "staff assistant" which will enable him to arrive at the vital planning decisions required in our "brave new world."

For generations, our colleagues in the field of journalism have been debating the issue of whether a newspaper should create or merely reflect the news. When this issue is applied to the field of planning, I have no hesitancy in suggesting that the planner must create, as well as reflect, the aspirations of the larger urban and regional community. If the planner merely reflects the existing values of his community in formulating decisions, he is restricting his function as a planner and failing to discharge his obligation to the clientele which he serves. Hopefully, decision-making theory will present the tools with which the planner can create the image of the future.

Chapter Twelve

Comprehensive Planning as a Field of Study

by Melville C. Branch

Assistant for Planning and Member of the Senior Staff (West Coast), Thompson Ramo Wooldridge Inc., Los Angeles

All too frequently the word planning is used so broadly that it is almost meaningless or so carelessly that it is confusing. We need to specify what kind of planning we have in mind in every instance. About a year ago, I had occasion to develop descriptions of different types of planning which are applicable to our subject here.[1]

The single word *planning* refers to any activity which seeks to achieve an objective in future time. It is thus a generic term with almost universal application.

Physical planning is concerned primarily with the characteristics and arrangement of three-dimensional features on the land. Although cost and many other considerations are always involved, spatial design is the central form of analysis and the end product is an areal

[1] Melville C. Branch, "The Corporate Planning Process—Plans, Decision, Implementation," *Operations Research*, VI, No. 4 (July-August, 1958), pp. 539-52.

pattern. Usually this work is performed by professional specialists called physical planners. Plans for the resolution of the financial, political, legal, and other problems implicit in such schemes are developed by others who are not titled planners as such. Physical planning is therefore a restrictive term describing a form of partial planning. City and regional planning are its best known applications.

Functional planning focuses on a particular aspect of the total problem, such as production scheduling or cash requirements in a business, highways or forest conservation in civil governmental planning, or airborne logistics or naval maneuver in military planning. Functional planning is essentially segmental in nature, although necessarily it must fit associated considerations. In colloquial terms, it may have to do with several related slices of the pie, or only a single thin slice intensively studied.

Comprehensive planning is the continued establishment of objectives for an institutional or organizational entity as a whole, and the conduct of its affairs so as to maximize the attainment of these goals. I refer to any organization, institution, or establishment with a sufficient degree of self-determination in its operations to make planning for its own future worth while. Examples would include: a business enterprise, a municipality, a governmental agency or military service, a university, a professional association—or any subordinate unit within these primary entities with a sufficient degree of autonomy.

Comprehensive planning seeks to optimize the total productive accomplishment and effective existence over time of the organism to which it is applied. It is therefore coordinative, inclusive, and projective in its viewpoint. As the descriptive adjective indicates, it is not limited to physical planning nor is it otherwise segmental in nature. In fact, one of the primary purposes of comprehensive planning is the integration of various functional and other partial planning activities. Specific examples on a large scale are: the Tennessee Valley project with its combination of flood control, navigation, land-use readjustment, community relocation, electric power generation and distribution, soil regeneration, and related manufacture; Operation Overlord for the invasion of Normandy by the combined allied military services during the Second World War; or the planning programs of such companies as Canadian Westinghouse or American Telephone and Telegraph. It is also applied by smaller or subordinate units to the full scope of their more limited activities.

The general terms *government planning, business* or *corporate planning,* and *military planning* refer to the application of the process within these areas of activity. It may be comprehensive in scope, functional in nature, or include physical planning. Similarly, different forms of planning are occasionally categorized by their primary characteristic or main objective, such as *socio-economic* or *social planning.* These particular terms have been somewhat in disrepute because of their identification with socialist or dictatorial governments, although planning of this general nature has existed for some time in our democratic society in the form of public health programs, social security, unemployment insurance, tax policies, fair employment practices, and the various regulatory activities of different levels of government.

Each of these types of planning is normally a different professional field of study, although there are important common denominators which will be mentioned later. Physical planning is taught in the graduate programs of twenty-five or more universities, usually associated with architectural or engineering schools.[2] Several of these have been in existence many years, with well-developed curricula. Ordinarily, graduates from these programs are employed by the municipal planning commissions and departments throughout the country, private consultant firms, or county, regional, and state planning agencies.[3]

Education in functional planning is part of the study of the parent field. Thus, financial planning is incorporated in the curricula of certain schools of finance or economics; industrial production or facilities planning in engineering; or war plans in military training. As one would expect, graduates who have been interested in the application of these fields to planning are to be found in private enterprise, civil government, the military services, or wherever their particular functional planning specialty is relevant.

To my knowledge, no educational program exists at the present time emphasizing comprehensive planning (as it is defined here) as a field of study. The last effort in this direction was The Program of Education and Research in Planning at the University of Chicago.[4]

If these are the basic kinds of planning activitiy and education, we should establish the prospects in general for the future before discussing planning as a field of study specifically. One of the consequences of my own experience in planning within a governmental agency, a university, and a business enterprise is the realization

2 "Special Report on Education," *Newsletter* (Chicago: American Society of Planning Officials, September, 1957), 4 pp.

3 *Handbook and Roster 1954* (Washington: American Institute of Planners), 55 pp.

4 Harvey S. Perloff, *Education for Planning: City, State, and Regional*, Part III, Education and Research in Planning: A Review of the University of Chicago Experiment (Published for Resources of the Future, Inc., by The Johns Hopkins Press, 1957), pp. 133-64.

that there are real and significant resistances to planning in this country—in both individuals and social organisms. Although we cannot deny rationally the logic of organized forethought, there are within us as human beings certain conscious and unconscious antipathies to planning and some of its implications for our lives.

I can illustrate this contention only very briefly here. There are strong emotional and physical investments in the status quo, a natural wish to leave well enough alone. The effectuation of planning requires changes in our institutions, new and different ways of doing things, organizational readjustments, a realignment of vested interests, and the displacement of people. Planning always involves conclusions and commitments with respect to the indefinite future. It is more difficult to plan than not to plan, seemingly easier to wait until the situation is self-evident and decisions are forced upon us.

Yet we are torn by an increasing desire for social security, a stabilized business cycle, and in general as little risk as possible—and this can only be achieved by anticipatory action. Perhaps most important of all, planning involves present sacrifice for future gain—the withdrawal from current use of a portion of the human and material resources available and its commitment for an expected benefit at some future time. There are basic psychological limitations on what people are able and willing to forego in the present for the benefits of succeeding generations.

We must recognize such reactions in our teaching of planning, its development as a field of study, in the formulation of practical plans, and their realistic implementation. They are limitations to be overcome rather than reasons not to proceed. There are trends in our society which suggest there are no alternatives to increased planning: the growing technological and organizational complexity of business and government, the expanding net of interaction between the multitude of different activities serving or influencing each other, population growth, the continuing specialization of labor and knowledge, or the foreseeable exhaustion or inadequacy of many of the natural energy resources on which we rely so heavily today. It should be emphasized this does not necessitate autocratic control or any fundamental change in our democratic way of life; quite the contrary, organized forethought may be crucial to our maintaining the essential individual and political freedoms.

If these conclusions are correct, there will be a continuing demand for people trained in physical planning; existing schools and departments will be expanded and new programs will be organized. An even greater growth can be expected in functional planning; the application of many of the functional fields to planning will be established as a specific concentration within appropriate university departments. Education for comprehensive planning is the greatest unfilled need at present and the most challenging opportunity for the future. To a large extent, the progress of both physical and functional planning will depend on the intellectual advance and successful application of comprehensive planning as the highest form and level of this activity. This implies that it is potentially an intellectual discipline or distinctive field of study.

It is my conviction that comprehensive planning will develop its own body of substantive knowledge. In fact, the tap roots for this advancement are already established and growing. Essentially, comprehensive planning is concerned with coordination and projection into the future. Although these most fundamental aspects can be expressed this simply, it is clear that a great

203

range, depth, and complexity of knowledge and activity are involved in the two words.

Coordination is correlation; and philosophy, physics, mathematics, engineering, economics, and all the other established disciplines have been deeply concerned with correlation since their inception. More recently, the terms systems approach and systems engineering have been widely used to describe the higher levels of coordi- nation required in complex groupings of many interde- pendent parts. These systems may involve, for example: weapons, communications, automatic controls, or groups of people—separately or in combination. They may com- prise a geographic, social, economic, political, organiza- tional, or institutional entity—such as a metropolitan city, space exploration, the federal government, or a business corporation. There are also, of course, purely intellectual systems in logic, mathematics, religion, or political philosophy.

In terms of its practical application, coordination in planning not only presents problems of mechanical or material interconnection, but also requires the correla- tion of highly disparate elements, the tangible and the intangible. As a single illustration, an industrial facility is composed of a multitude of physical and material ele- ments which are considered and correlated, integrated into a design solution, and translated into three-dimen- sions. If we extend this correlation to a higher level for more comprehensive corporate planning purposes, a new set of financial, psychological, and human engineer- ing elements is introduced which we cannot now inte- grate by scientific analysis. This limitation leaves very important questions to be answered by the most ap- proximate judgments or intuitions. How does one dem- onstrate the value to a business of a window and exterior outlook for professional employees—especially if it means the postponement of some fringe benefit? At what density of occupancy is productivity maximized? What provisions for the future rearrangement of space are justified in the light of either their immediate dollar costs or the sacrifice of an optimum environment for the purposes at hand? Above the essential requirements, what additional capital expenditures for higher quality or aesthetic features in a physical facility are a sound investment over time?

Projection is also an objective common to most areas of endeavor. A major concern of intellectual fields in general is to develop knowledge which can be applied today to be of benefit at some future time. For example, a measurement of success in science is the capacity to predict. The word planning in itself connotes this primary characteristic. Some extrapolations are made with high reliability by established analytical methods. Others, of course, can only be made within a range of variation, and a third category of projections must be based on subjective judgment, intuition, or occasionally guess.

It must be recognized, however, that in comprehensive planning long-range reliable prediction is by no means essential to success. Of greater significance is the regular reporting of recent history, the current situation, and the present trend extrapolated a short time into the future. With these regularly-revised, shorter-range projections, the lead-time for advance planning and action is reduced but the reliability of the forecast is increased. If the comprehensive planning program is organized for rapid revision, and the short-range adjustment of operations is possible and worth while, the basic function and benefits of the process are realized. Naturally, the longer-range, more reliable, and comprehensive the projections, the more definite planning can be.

There are aspects of most organisms which can be forecast accurately well into the future, others which can be extended only a short span. Corporations have long-term debts representing financial commitments which can be extrapolated within relatively narrow limits, whereas accurate longer-range sales forecasts may be out of the question. Some natural phenomena such as tree growth, silting, erosion, or radioactivity can be anticipated quite precisely under certain conditions, but the unpredictability of many floods, fires, pestilence, or other "acts of God" is signified in the descriptive term. Individual consumer demand for power or water in a city can be forecast more reliably than its over-all growth or the form and precise direction of its physical development. In military planning, the lead-time from development to operational status for a new aircraft can be forecast quite accurately, but an achievement in basic research involving an intellectual breakthrough cannot. My point here is simply to emphasize that projection is a universal and complex activity, involving past experience, mathematical and statistical probability, other forms of analytical extrapolation, subjective judgment, and preconscious intuition or reasoning.

Besides coordination and projection, there are other general characteristics of comprehensive planning, whether it is applied to business, government, or military matters. I will not attempt to describe these characteristics, but only refer to an illustrative few in a word or two and leave their interpretation to your imagination: flexibility; time and degree of commitment; plans or planning; consideration of alternatives; safety factor; foci of single- or multiple-function emphasis; psychological factors; or optimum allocation of available resources over time.

It is in connection with such types of general intellectual problems that I believe comprehensive planning will gradually acquire a unique body of knowledge. Being a composite or integrative field, like engineering, sociology, or political science, it cannot intrinsically have the same kind of uniqueness as the fundamental intellectual disciplines or those fields which are narrow in scope. But in the same sense biochemistry or biophysics produce knowledge beyond what they derive from their parent fields, comprehensive planning should also make its own distinctive intellectual contribution.

Trends in this direction seem to me already apparent in the systems approach developing within a number of fields, in information and decision theory, game theory, symbolic logic, the psychology of groups, operations research techniques, data processing, quality control, or dynamic financial accounting. There is also experimentation with certain specific mechanisms closely related to comprehensive planning: planning control rooms, data-processing centers, computer simulation of military and business situations and executive decision-making, or more inclusive analogues facilitating and extending architectural-engineering design in physical planning. In my opinion, these developments will be synthesized and crystallized in comprehensive planning because, as pointed out previously, this is the common-denominator field representing and encompassing many crucial areas of practical need and application. Incidentally, another expression may become the accepted term to describe the process I call comprehensive planning; "systems engineering" or "management science" are two distinct possibilities.

Figure 1 illustrates graphically the trend of intellectual disciplines and professional fields toward a substantive body of systems—or comprehensive—planning theory, principles, and methodology which will apply to

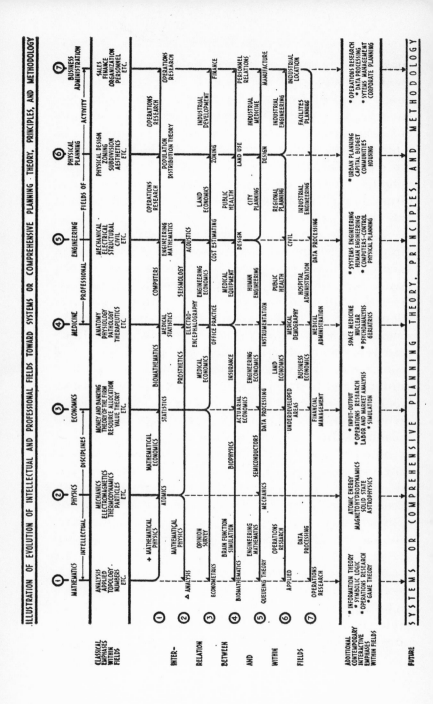

ILLUSTRATION OF EVOLUTION OF INTELLECTUAL AND PROFESSIONAL FIELDS TOWARD SYSTEMS OR COMPREHENSIVE PLANNING THEORY, PRINCIPLES, AND METHODOLOGY

many areas of endeavor. Following the vertical downward from each of the seven fields at the top, it will be noted at the bottom of the chart that each has broadened in scope, and several are developing similar approaches or even the same emphasis. Thus, Operations Research is found as a contemporary concentration at the bottom under Mathematics, Economics, and Business Administration; it could also have been included under Engineering. Although selected as an example only under Economics, Simulation in its various forms is today an important emphasis within many fields. And Urban Planning is now a professional and educational interest of Engineering, Architecture, Geography, Sociology, and Economics—as well as the principal concern of Physical Planning. Those contemporary emphases marked with an asterisk seem most likely to contribute to the intellectual development of comprehensive planning as a distinctive field.

In the middle section of the chart, interrupting each vertical from the seven fields at the top, are subordinate concentrations which relate directly to others of these primary fields. To illustrate specifically, if we follow the horizontal line marked number one emanating from Mathematics, and pause at each arrowhead as we proceed to the right, we find Mathematics represented in Atomics under Physics, Statistics under Economics, Medical Statistics under Medicine, Engineering Mathematics under Engineering, Population Distribution Theory under Physical Planning, and Operations Research under Business Administration.

Also in the middle section of Figure 1, between the verticals extending down from the seven fields, are examples of the so-called "bridging" fields, which involve the synthesis or interaction of two or more of the primary specializations. To illustrate again with Mathematics, if we follow the same horizontal line marked number one and observe between each arrowhead, we find Mathematics linked with Physics by Mathematical Physics, with Economics by Mathematical Economics, Medicine by Biomathematics, Engineering by Computers, and with Physical Planning and Business Administration by Operations Research. Clearly, composite fields are becoming more numerous and repetitive in the over-all pattern of intellectual development. No attempt has been made to include all such fields or the subordinate concentrations; additional examples will undoubtedly occur to the reader.

If comprehensive planning is indeed potentially a field of knowledge and study, educational efforts must be inaugurated to teach what is known, and to conduct and stimulate research. My own participation in planning programs at two universities indicates there are several important requirements for the successful establishment of a graduate program which will include or feature comprehensive planning.

As described here, comprehensive planning is too new and insufficiently recognized to comprise a direct means of livelihood for a substantial number of people at the present time. Although this situation is changing, it will be some years before comprehensive planning is identified per se, with a consequent demand for persons trained specifically in this discipline. In the beginning, therefore, it will be necessary to provide basic professional education in a type or application of planning for which there is a definite demand and specific employment opportunities after graduation. Comprehensive planning would be included in the program to the extent feasible at first, and would become an increasingly large part of the curriculum until in time it was the primary emphasis. The number of institutions providing graduate education in comprehensive planning will, of course, be determined ultimately by our societal development and its demand for such training.

To survive, such a planning program or school must have solid support. Until it has had time to prove itself and become established, it needs a mentor and strong advocate. It can be incorporated within or closely associated with the most appropriate department or school, but energetic and continued backing must be assured. Otherwise, when departmental budgets are cut or the demands upon available funds are heavy, it is only natural that the requirements of the department host will be given precedence over those of the foster child. If established independently within the university, the backing of the president, other chief executive, or trustees must be certain for the same reason. If foundation or other support could be obtained for five years, the planning program should be able to insure its own survival by the end of this period.

However, it is established that the planning program should cooperate with and serve other university departments. In this way, an understanding of planning is furthered and mutually beneficial ties are created which hopefully will engender support from the associated units in their own self-interest. Research should be a strong emphasis not only because it is required for the advancement of comprehensive planning as a field, but because grants are of course supportive in a practical way of the educational program itself. Close and active contacts with business and industry, government, and other outside planning efforts are important because they are intellectually stimulating in general and specifically suggestive, and can lead to unforeseen support in time of need.

Needless to say, the selection of the faculty is of fundamental importance. Not only must its members possess the requisite knowledge and ability to teach, but creative minds and a keen research interest are required to advance our substantive understanding of comprehensive planning and its techniques of accomplishment. Also, since planning as a field of endeavor is a consequence of recognized problems and will continue tied to its application in real life, practical experience provides a background comprehension for which there is no satisfactory academic substitute. New theoretical constructs concerning comprehensive planning will be formulated, but this body of theory will be superior in itself and more useful in practice if it is rooted in the realities of the human-physical environmental situation which is both its *raison d'ê'tre* and end application.

In closing, let me recapitulate my main points:

1. The different kinds of planning must be identified if we are to progress intellectually and educationally.

2. Comprehensive planning is the continued establishment of objectives for an institutional or organizational entity as a whole, and the conduct of its affairs so as to maximize the attainment of these goals.

3. The trends of our society will require more planning.

4. Additional programs in all types of planning education will therefore be needed.

5. As the highest form and level of planning activity, comprehensive planning constitutes the greatest educational challenge and opportunity.

6. There are indications it will become a distinctive discipline and field of study.

7. Educational programs in comprehensive planning are not likely to succeed unless—

a) for the present, they include professional training in functional or other applications of planning which provide a means of livelihood;
b) there is active and continued financial support during the initial years;
c) cooperative ties with other university units and the outside world are established;
d) research is a strong emphasis;
e) the faculty is superior in knowledge, teaching ability, and capacity for creative research.

Notes from the Discussion Period

Question: I am concerned about the relation of developing an intellectual discipline of comprehensive planning and a realistic educational curriculum—for example, within the School of Public and International Affairs here at the University of Pittsburgh. To what extent should we attempt to contribute to such a development, or rely on its becoming available to us over time from research in a variety of other fields?

Dr. Branch: If the conclusion expressed in my presentation is correct, the program would provide professional training for which there is an established demand. It would also include as much education in comprehensive planning as feasible, so that graduates would not only benefit in general from this broader background, but could more likely gradually extend the horizions of the limited or partial planning activity in which they would probably first be engaged as professionals.

Ultimately, as research in comprehensive planning theory, principles, and methodology advances, and as the societal trends which I mentioned earlier establish their roles in the successful management of operating organizations, supply and demand for persons trained in comprehensive planning per se will approach a balance.

My own estimate is that will be achieved within the next fifteen years—possibly ten years.

I do not believe you can simply rely on other fields to perform the research and accomplish the intellectual breakthroughs on which your own advancement in substantive understanding depends. There must be some indigenous effort within the planning program itself. Only in this way can other fields be stimulated to extend their contributions to planning. And research grants and the better students are certainly more likely to be attracted to the educational program which is actively trying to advance its own knowledge. Perhaps most important, no one else can be expected to have as clear a concept of the potentialities and requirements of comprehensive planning as a distinct discipline as the educational program in planning which is interested in extending its own intellectual frontiers in this way. You cannot expect others to do your own fundamental thinking for you; they, of course, have their own exploratory thinking to do.

From a practical point of view, how much effort is expended on basic research and how many courses are provided today in a form of planning which will not be practiced widely for some years to come depends on a balance within the total educational time available between the courses required for employment in planning as it is now and those which will assist the graduate to compete and contribute as his field develops.

There appears to me little question that comprehensive planning is the stimulating prospect around the corner. There are many signs in the wind: the growth of systems engineering, more inclusive military planning, operations research, activity in decision-making theory and the simulation of executive management situations for research and training purposes, the interest in mathematical game and communication theory, or symbolic logic.

Question: I am wondering if comprehensive planning is a potential discipline and therefore appropriately included in education, or whether it is simply the product of the intellectual ability of the individual. If so, scholars are born and not made.

Dr. Branch: I think it has been established that intellectual ability is not born. Intelligence, we know, is influenced by hereditary factors, but intelligence and intellectual ability are not synonymous. The latter is greatly influenced by environment in general, education in particular, and the psychological characteristics of the individual. Nor are scholars born, unless we assume that the entire post-natal psychological environment and experience have no effect on the development of their academic potentialities and their choice to become scholars in fact. And this I do not believe.

I would certainly agree that you cannot make a silk-purse scholar out of a sow's-ear individual. There are persons who do not possess the requisite intellectual capabilities for comprehensive planning because of limited mental endowment at birth. There are also persons emotionally unsuited to the planning profession. But this, of course, is true in other fields as well.

Question: Will the student in comprehensive planning study mathematics and statistics?

Dr. Branch: Yes, I am sure the mathematical disciplines will play a more important role than they have to date in physical planning. Linear programming, communication and game theory, symbolic logic, or mathematical models are important from both theoretical and practical viewpoints. It will usually not be necessary or feasible for the planning professional to be expert at mathematics, but he should certainly acquire a more extensive working knowledge than most of us in the field now have. It is becoming a more important and common language or form of expression, and is being used more extensively as a working tool.

Question: Can one specialize in generalization, or is generalization a specialty?

Dr. Branch: First, we must indicate what we mean by specialization and generalization. To me, specialization means concentration on particular subject matter. Normally, this refers to a certain discipline, or an area within a field. We usually think of the super-specialist as intensely knowledgeable within a very narrow range. To illustrate, I have known a professor who spent his entire adult life studying termites—and a fascinating and useful study it was.

The generalist applies the same capacity of retained knowledge broadly rather than narrowly. His area of knowledge can be visualized as a horizontal band covering the different aspects of a single field (for example, the systems engineer) or of several fields (business administration), as compared with the vertical band of knowledge of the specialist extending from a single subject or phase but including great depth rather than breadth of information. Neither the systems engineer nor the business administrator is expected to know thoroughly all the subject matter of the different component fields involved, but rather how to better interrelate these areas of specialization which are closely tied together in most real life situations.

All scholars are, of course, both specialists and generalists in that even the narrowest specialist must look inclusively at the different elements with which he is concerned. So far, no ultimate or indivisible particle or unity of knowledge has been found. The specialist is interrelating very precise or even minute elements, rather than the broad aspects or entire fields which are the concern of the generalists, but in this exact sense he is also acting as a generalist. Both generalization and specialization are inherent in any study—in our cogitative processes of analysis and deduction. Referring back to our visualization a few moments ago, the specialist generalizes "vertically," the generalist "horizontally."

Based on this reasoning, my answer is yes: one can "specialize in generalization" or "generalization is a specialty." Or as a teacher of mine used to phrase it, one can be "a specialist at not being a specialist." But I prefer the use of different descriptive phrases which do not use words which suggest contradictions in themselves. I would say rather: there are areas of knowledge and important contributions in real life which emphasize the interrelationships between and synthesis of different fields or specializations. It happens that our substantive knowledge of generalization in this integrative sense is at present in its infancy compared with the depth of knowledge established within narrower concentrations. But as pointed out in my presentation, I think this discrepancy will be significantly reduced within the next ten years or so.

Dr. Perloff: There is a tendency in most fields of study to seek integrative approaches. In the case of civil engineering, for example, some serious probing in this direction is taking place by way of systems analysis or systems engineering.

In public administration—which at one time was more narrowly concerned with personnel, purchasing, budgets and the like—"administrative management" has come to the fore as an approach which looks to the integration of the separate administrative facets and emphasizes the projective aspect of what policy and actions today mean for tomorrow.

In architecture, there was a time when buildings were considered independently from all but their immediate surroundings. As the facts and attitudes of our physical existence on the land changed over the years, it became clear that individual buildings had to be considered in a broader context. Among many other things, the mere fact that the utilities and servicing of a building are not self-sufficient but dependent on an area-wide system led to the consideration, first, of the subdivision or neighborhood and then to city planning.

In each of these three examples, and for many other fields as well, the context is broadening and efforts are being made to achieve greater elements of integration for the field. These efforts are called by different names, but they are essentially the same ln purpose. The question is whether a separate intellectual discipline will develop which focuses on this integrative function.

This question is of direct interest to us from an educational viewpoint. If this integrative knowledge is in process of formulation, to what extent can and should the work underway be included in the curriculum and research of a university planning program today? It seems to me that the trend is sufficiently clear, the work accomplished of adequate importance, and the future significance of this coordinative approach such, that at least one course, seminar, or workshop on comprehensive planning might well be included in a planning curriculum.

Question: What would happen if you brought different specialists together in an attempt to advance the knowledge and techniques of systems analysis or comprehensive planning? Some would understand mathematical statements, others would not. They might find it difficult to communicate with each other. Could something new or productive come from such a gathering?

Dr. Branch: I think we can agree that such conferences would be for research purposes—at least for some time to come. Later, they might be incorporated into the curriculum as a stimulus or demonstration.

Although one cannot predict with certainty, such work sessions should be productive. If communication is indeed difficult or even impossible, this is most important to know for it will then be necessary to agree on an optimum common-denominator form of communication, and the different specialities will express their contributions in this way. It may be necessary to devise a new means of conceptualization or statement.

In a series of integrative work sessions, it should be possible to delineate the major interactions between fields, develop a construct or formulation which will portray at least the more vital of these connections, and finally derive an analogue or simulation useful for comprehensive planning purposes. The effort itself would undoubtedly prove stimulating to all concerned, and provide a worthwhile cross-fertilization of information, ideas, techniques, research, and thoughts of the future.

Much would depend on the selection of the participants. Besides his knowledge and professional capability, each representative of a field would be familiar with scientific method and acquainted with the "systems concept." He would concentrate during each work session on its purposes, rather than upon any special subjective interests or attitudes less directly relevant.

Yes, I think such an effort would be productive.

Comment and Question: What Dr. Branch has said about comprehensive planning, Mr. Fagin applied to the planning function in public agencies. The similarity of their concepts leads us to consider, first, how these concepts influence planning education, and second, what they imply concerning the functions of a central planning staff within government.

Planning is the means of utilizing all applicable information to develop policy objectives and ways of achieving them. In government, there is a division of labor between a central planning agency and the planning functions of various departments or satellites (as Mr. Fagin has called them).

To what extent does the central planning agency utilize special knowledge from outside and draw upon specialists from other fields?

Dr. Branch: In any central or comprehensive planning activity—be it government or business—the knowledge and judgment of many people working with different or subordinate organizations are needed. The staff group engaged in comprehensive planning does not attempt to analyze the many different objectives and ways of achieving them from their own heads alone. Such an effort would not only be the antithesis of the coordinative planning process as I see it, but in most cases would be doomed to failure from the beginning. Comprehensive planning is correlation at the top, the integration of particular objectives and courses of action which are formulated initially by those responsible for each such phase of the total effort. The task of comprehensive planning is to organize these component contributions into an over-all strategy and plan of action for the organism as a whole—consistent with its broader objectives, potentialities, and limitations.

Usually, the plans of different departments or associated units necessarily represent a segmental rather than an over-all viewpoint. As a single example, they may separately suggest expenditures which, when totaled, are beyond the capacity of the parent or controlling organization to produce.

In any planning activity of even moderate size and complexity, expert knowledge from the outside is usually needed. Not many activities of any sort today can hope to have available within themselves the full scope of knowledge and information they require to derive the best solution or series of actions for the future. Outside contributions are often sought to fill a particular need. They are compared with other inputs and considerations, and are represented in the final planning conclusions in their proper relation and proportion.

Question: In this case, is not planning closely akin to management?

Dr. Branch: Very much so—if we add the adjective "enlightened" to "management." Although I use the words comprehensive planning to describe the activity we are discussing here today, management science and systems engineering are terms also used for essentially the same process. One of these terms may become the accepted descriptive tag rather than comprehensive planning.

Question: How can you educate for comprehensive planning at a single institution and still call it comprehensive planning?

Dr. Branch: I think we have a confusion of both terms and concepts. If I understand your question correctly, you are asking how can you educate in a single place for an endeavor which by definition involves too many different activities and fields of knowledge to be supplied at one location.

We are doing it all the time. For example, no school of business administration can encompass within itself or the university of which it is part all the intellectual concentrations or professional specializations which are applied in the successful management of a corporation—within itself, its community, and the larger contexts with which it is related economically, competitively, legally, governmentally, and in many other ways. Nor can a single program of training in command include the full range of military activities and specific knowledge involved. But the existence and continued growth of such educational programs indicates there are attitudes, approaches, facts, and techniques of administration and coordinative direction which are useful and can be taught. Of course, no curriculum is (or should attempt to be) self-sufficient; that is why we have visiting lecturers.

With reference to the second part of your question: How can you call it comprehensive planning if everything is not conceptually included or covered in course work? The word comprehensive is not used to imply total knowledge or universal comprehension, which of course cannot exist in any individual. It denotes only that this type of planning has to do with the over-all objectives and plans for an organism or activity as a whole, and not some particular or perhaps highly specialized part of it. To use a rough analogy, the view is wide-angle toward the whole forest and not telescopic toward the trees.

Question: Do you assume operations research techniques will be used in comprehensive planning, and will other fields be able to use them also?

Dr. Branch: Yes, indeed. Operations Research has been described as "an analytic method of studying the operation of a system and an integrated set of actions." Usually, it is conducted by a team of specialists in different fields. It employs mathematical analysis, seeks underlying principles, and derives conclusions which indicate the probable results of various courses of action. Its most useful application is in complex problems which can be measured and described in quantitative terms.

You can see from this that Operations Research is very similar in its approach and general method to what we call comprehensive planning. If Operations Research as a field broadens to encompass the intangible, imponderable, indefinite, and unquantifiable—then it will become practically synonymous with comprehensive planning, management science, systems engineering, or whatever the generally accepted label turns out to be. All of these areas of interest and activity are trending in the same direction toward a similar intellectual objective—namely, to apply rational processes, scientific method, and the newer technological developments (such as analogue and digital computers) to the better direction of complex activities or systems.

My personal opinion is that Operations Research is at present seriously limited by its own self-imposed criteria of numerical expression and consistency and mathematical treatment. There are many vital parts of any over-all management situation which we are not going to be able to solve with numbers for a long time to come. The most obvious of these is people: the emotional, unpredictable, changing, irrational side which exists in all of us. And coupled with this to make it even more difficult, is our proper insistence in a democratic society that the maximum of free will and individual freedom be retained. So, I see Operations Research (as it is now) performing a valuable role of special, partial, and precise analysis within the more inclusive context of comprehensive planning. Some of its techniques will be modified or extended for direct use in the comprehensive planning process itself, and it will continue to contribute to other fields—engineering, economics, business administration, manufacturing, or military logistics, to name but a few.

Question: What do you think is the role of the design skills in systems analysis or comprehensive planning?

Dr. Branch: It depends on how you define design. I assume you mean the areal arrangement of different activities, functions, and features on the land—included in education for physical planning, architecture, civil engineering, landscape architecture, or geography.

Such design training is valuable in several ways. Clearly, it is useful in physical planning which is concerned with land use, zoning, communities, circulation, or other areal problems and solutions. It is also valuable in a more general way. Having to identify the elements and considerations involved and their various interrelationships constitutes an instructive exercise in problem delineation, analysis, and programming. The exercise is realistic and practical in that there are either the limitations imposed by the physical and socio-economic facts of the existing area selected for study, or a hypothetical situation can easily be devised to simulate the conditions of real life.

At the same time, the possibility of enough change can be assumed to permit the application of theory and creative imagination. Such training demonstrates preparatory analysis, correlation, an examination of alternatives, choice and decision, projection into the future, the characteristics of the desirable solution, the necessity of compromise between the ideal and achievable, and other significant lessons to be learned in planning education. It promotes an approach to problem situations and a capacity to find and program feasible solutions, which are not restricted to three-dimensional matters.

We should note that the term design is much broader

than its specific meaning for physical planners, architects, or civil engineers. There is design in the development of a computer, accounting system, metropolitan government, mathematical formulation, optimum strategy, schedule of coordinated action, and many other creative accomplishments not in themselves three-dimensional. Design is by no means the exclusive province of the spatially-oriented, as they sometimes seem to suggest.

To finally answer your question: spacial design has an essential role in physical planning. Design in the more inclusive sense is equally essential in any form of planning. After all, any plan is a program of action toward established objectives, and it must be studied, shaped, tested, and finally expressed or conceptualized—and design (call it by another name, if you will) is inherent in this process of development. Whether some physical design training should be included in comprehensive planning education, I don't know at the moment. I have not had the occasion to try and think it through. I would imagine, however, that an exposure to spatial design problems, concepts, and solutions will always be required—for the simple reason that most plants (if not all of them) are ultimately expressed in some three-dimensional form or effect within the spatial world in which we live. And it may be that exercises in physical planning design are a good intellectual introduction to design in its more inclusive sense.

Chapter Thirteen

Planning Education and Research:
A Summary Statement

by Harvey S. Perloff

Director, Program of Regional Studies, Resources for the Future,
Inc., Washington, D.C.

By way of summary, it might be asked: What is the
potential role for planning education and research in
the academic world and in the world of practical affairs?

The essays presented before the University of Pitts-
burgh-Carnegie Institute of Technology Planning Seminar both explicitly and implicitly stressed the open-
ended possibilities for contribution by the planning
field to a wide range of subjects and activities.

Planning in the United States is over fifty years old
and yet all the participants could give the impression
that they were talking about something quite new, something for the future, rather than something about the
past and present. And it is significant that men from so
many different fields could all approach the central
issues of planning as of concern to themselves and to
their fields. Thus, throughout, one finds phases like
"we should," "we will have to," "we must," "we need

to." Surprisingly, there was nothing like the old expression, "Why don't *they?*"

Everyone involved seemed to accept the idea that it is for us—here and now—to tackle the tough urban problems that lie ahead of us, and to try to do something about realizing the potentialities that are inherent in the planning approach and in planning education and research. The behavioral scientist, observing this phenomenon, might well say: "This is not at all surprising. Planning attracts the hopeful, up-beat type of person who can be expected to look to the future to want to do something about the problems we face." This is very true. As a matter of fact, it is precisely *because* of the special orientation of planning that it holds out such tremendous potentialities in both education and practical affairs.

The progress made in education and research within most of the scientific and technical fields at our universities has been achieved at a certain cost. Abstraction, the narrowing of subject matter, and endless refinement have been essential—and inevitable—ingredients of progress in these academic fields. Even fields like sociology and philosophy, which traditionally have had great breadth and a humanistic foundation, have been succumbing lately to the pressures of academic advance by way of abstraction and narrow specialization.

Actually, of course, each of the social science disciplines, and fields such as architecture and engineering, have been much concerned with the question of how to develop a broad view of human behavior and of the relationship between people and physical environment. They have also been concerned with possible contributions to the development of sensible public policy for the solution of social problems. However, the individual scholars who want to contribute to these significant endeavors find great barriers. The organization of an interdisciplinary effort in either education or research with colleagues from other disciplines is found to be a time-consuming and difficult matter. They soon discover that interdisciplinary research has its own severe requirements and that they would have to devote many years to learning their way around in this difficult type of endeavor. When they reach out beyond analysis into policy questions, they find that there is only too often a storm of protest from their colleagues about the "unscientific" nature of their work. Also, aside from a few fields such as public administration and business administration, the scholar who wants to work closely with practical affairs, either in government or with private organizations, tends to find it extremely difficult to lay out fruitful lines of contact where he can make useful contribution without being swallowed up by the demands of the difficult day-by-day current practical problems.

The scholar who has experienced difficulties of this type is likely to come to the conclusion that, if he wishes to contribute directly to the solution of complex social problems, he really needs help on two scores. First, he needs a well-established framework within which interdisciplinary research and education can be carried out. And he needs organized channels through which ideas can flow, fruitfully and cumulatively. Secondly, he finds that he needs "legitimization"; that is, he needs a well-recognized reason for devoting himself to applied problems and to policy questions and an accepted and organized basis for working productively with persons in the field of practical affairs.

Several of the academic fields—for example, public and business administration—have been quite successful in establishing some of these conditions, but, few other fields of study hold out so effective a framework for achieving all of these ends as does the field of urban planning. It is precisely here that some of the greatest potentialities for planning lie. But there are implications involved which some of the planners themselves miss; namely, the full potentialities of planning can only be achieved by establishing very intimate links of planning with the various social science disciplines and the various related professional fields, particularly architecture, landscape architecture, engineering, public health, and law. Against this background, it can be seen that many of the concrete suggestions presented in the essays in this volume are directly pertinent and of immediate practical significance.

I find that the major ideas concerning potentialities for the future can be summarized under three main headings. These are not to be taken as tight compartments, but rather as ways of organizing complex ideas and suggestions.

The first of the broad categories focuses directly on education and research: the creation of a better *understanding* of man, society, and the physical environment. The second category covers policy formulation and creative design, involving both physical and social design. The third broad category deals with what might be called administration and execution; the "doing" phase as compared to the "understanding" phase as such. These various groups are interconnected, of course, in many ways.

Under the first category—which is concerned with education and research to broaden and deepen our understanding of man and environment—we find the various speakers referring to a wide variety of subjects the probing of which could logically be under the sponsorship of a planning group. It is interesting to note that

the strongest statements of the desirability of cooperative research under the sponsorship of a planning program came from the persons who themselves are working
within the individual disciplines outside of planning.
Taken all together, the speakers set down a list of research ideas which could keep a large group of our
best minds busy for a very long period of time. I can
do no more than refer to two or three examples of the
type of understanding which these men felt we need
urgently to develop.

Holmes Perkins posed a critical issue for study: How
do people want to live? Quite a few of the speakers
raised the same question, not surprisingly, since this is
central to much of the planning endeavor. Perkins
asked the further question, addressed to scholars in general: How do we go about finding out how people want
to live? Bogue anticipated this question when he
pointed out that we do not have much knowledge about
values, biases, and prejudices in predicting human re-
sponses to social and environmental changes. He pointed
out that planners should be encouraging more research
in this direction.

Richard Meier also stressed the importance of coming
to understand more about personal preferences, including those related to leisure time activities. The rates of
change here are very great, he pointed out, and therefore
directly affect the whole urban organization. Research
on leisure time activities can be related to questions
concerning services and facilities—such as parks and
recreation centers—and to movements of persons, and
therefore offer an intriguing way of getting at the whole
complex of factors involved in the urban organism.

The speakers pointed not only to significant areas of
planning-oriented research in relation to behavioral
aspects, but also pointed to needed areas for research

with regard to materials and physical processes. Thomas Stelson outlined new areas for cooperative research dealing with materials and energy, including analyses of the implications of new materials and new methods of using materials, and of ways of injecting the new knowledge into the administrative and political streams.

The second broad category of potentialities for planning study are related to policy formulation and creative design. Both Dean Stone and Dean Rice addressed themselves to what they could see as a great opportunity for a planning program. Dean Stone pointed out, for example, that in administration, the definition of objectives is the least developed and most overlooked task of all. Persons with training in both city planning and administration had much to contribute to the improvement of "management" in our communities. Dean Rice referred to the great potential role for persons with a feeling for creative design.

In addition, one might refer to the joint opportunity for advances along the lines of creative design and policy formulation. This, it seems to me, deserves a good bit of attention. The definitions of political objectives in the past have rarely had any design component attached to them, while design has so often been in a vacuum, disregarding human values, costs, and political processes. It may be at just this very point that planning has the greatest of all its opportunities, by making it possible for designers, scholars, administrators, and others to address themselves unashamedly to methods for evolving a better and more desirable future, including a more desirable physical environment for urban living.

That good design is a central issue for city planning was made clear by the speakers at the last session of the seminar. Dean Rice summarized the idea sharply when he said: "Planning should insist on positive esthetic solutions to every problem it considers." Dr. Walter Hovey added: "The town planner must have an awareness and sympathy for the point of view that accepts beauty as an objective." The thing to note is that the planner is in a position to press such a concept to the forefront of developmental policy, by bringing together the various skills so that "positive esthetic solutions" (to use Dean Rice's term) become possible. No one group can do this alone. Henry Fagin, John Howard, and Holmes Perkins, in their own ways, pointed to the same need for a close working together of various skills and groups. The architect, Holmes pointed out for example, simply cannot go about borrowing shapes, but rather he must adapt them to function. And to determine function is a role for all professions and not that of architecture alone. Thus, unless all are operating together, he suggested, creative urban design is not possible.

C. K. Yang, professor, department of sociology, University of Pittsburgh, on reviewing Donald Bogue's paper, underlined the same idea in yet another way when he pointed to the desirability of developing new working relationships between physical and social planning, so that the process moving through analysis, design, implementation, and evaluation is continuous rather than compartmentalized, coherent rather than disjointed and even internally in conflict.

Edward Smuts pointed to yet another relationship, that of urban physical design and economic patterns, and the mutual need for working through both of them for the creation of flexible arrangements which can avoid obsolescence and early decay. Herbert Simon and Glenn Ferguson both discussed the necessity not only for evolving fresh, uninhibited solutions for urban problems, but also the need for developing more public understanding and support of basic principles, which apply in improvement of the city. Creativeness without public support for the new ideas can turn out to be a sterile exercise and a highly frustrating one. Speaker after speaker stressed the point that true creativeness is an essential ingredient of the search for a better life.

In general, in the various papers, one finds as clear a statement as is to be found anywhere in the literature on the potentialities of planning study as a way of stimulating and channeling creative work with regard to developmental policy and design solutions for our urban problems.

The third broad category to which I have referred centers on the relation between planning and administration, or more broadly conceived, the relation of planning and the world of practical affairs. The social sciences and the technical sciences are, of course, in the final analysis, concerned directly with the world of practical affairs. And yet, as all those who have tried it know, it is no simple matter for the university scholar to work fruitfully with the persons in the field who have the day by day responsibility for administration either in public or private organizations. The special advantages which planning holds out for a fruitful relationship between "gown and town" arise in large part from the fact that planning is, in rather a unique way, consciously and consistently concerned with the relationship between substantive problems and substantive information, on the one side, and processes or procedures, on the other.

Take the case of the demographer who is concerned with the application of his particular knowledge and methods to the problems of the city. In planning, he will find a direct channel by which advances he makes can be directly applied in furthering the work of public agencies. It is no accident that sociologists like Donald Bogue are working very closely with planning agencies and with professional planners. They find in the planning field an unusual receptivity for research as a critical factor in practical operations.

The same is true of the economist who is interested in urban economics. He will find the practicing planner not only receptive to his new findings, but actually pushing him to move more rapidly in deepening our understanding of the economy of the urban region. It is no accident, for example, that it was the Pittsburgh Regional Planning Association that should have been the sponsor of the Pittsburgh economic study or the New York Regional Plan Association the sponsor of the New York region economic study.

It is interesting to note how many of the speakers in the seminar stressed the potentialities, by way of planning efforts, for improving our methods for arriving at community decisions and carrying them out so as to achieve our major community objectives. Each one of them saw this as a cooperative effort in which the social scientists, architects, engineers, and planners and the men of practical affairs would join hands to create new and better processes and political forms. Thus, Fritz Gutheim referred to the challenge to create new political forms to deal with what he called the "metropolitan agenda." Henry Fagin pointed to the potential role of planning in strengthening the structure of the executive branch. He presented the concept of planning as synonymous with the total staff function. Donald Stone, James Norton, John J. Matthews, Herbert Simon, and J. Steele Gow showed that some of the most intriguing questions in public administration center on the very issues with which planning is so centrally concerned. As a group, the speakers with a background in political science and public administration showed that they were much intrigued with the potentialities for both improving our knowledge and improving actual practice by way of a joining of forces of planning and public administration.

Melville C. Branch pointed to the intriguing possibilities inherent in the study of what he calls "comprehensive planning" as an approach and methodology which can be employed by an institutional or organizational entity.

These then are a few of the potentialities for planning as seen by the participants in the seminar.

Planning offers certain kinds of advantages that can be built upon. The fact is that planning practice urgently needs answers to questions concerning ways of making social decisions more rational and of projecting and studying the future. Thus, if a planning school does its job well, its faculty can be expected to become directly involved with precisely these questions. Possibly the most unique feature of planning study is the conscious consideration of the desirable and possible, as well as the existing and probable. The practical problems with which professional planners have to struggle serve to define the questions for planning education and research, so that in an appropriate academic environment such education and research would tend to bring useful new perspective to the study of social man and his environment. What we have then is an enterprise which can have real meaning only when it results in a joining of forces of many disciplines and fields of study, and only when it retains close and meaningful ties with the world of practical affairs.

Planning and the Urban Community

was designed by Mr. Jack W. Stauffacher, Department of Graphic Arts, Carnegie Institute of Technology. The book was set in linotype Baskerville, printed on Perkins & Squier RR Wove, and bound in Bancroft's Arrestox C by the American Book-Stratford Press, Inc., of New York. The dust jackets were printed from Mr. Stauffacher's design by William G. Johnston Co., of Pittsburgh.

Fifteen hundred copies have been published in this first edition under the joint imprints of Carnegie Institute of Technology and the University of Pittsburgh.

Date Due